# THE 10

# AMAZING

# STEPS TO SUCCESS!

How to achieve your goals and live
happily.

The ULTIMATE

step by step strategy guide

to reach your goals!

Cristian Cairo

Printed in Great Britain for 'The 10 Amazing Steps to Success–How to Achieve your Goals and Live Happily!' by Cristian Cairo.

Every effort has been made to ensure that the information in this book is correct at the time of publication. The author Cristian Cairo and the publisher do not assume and hereby disclaim any liability to any party for any loss, damage, or disruption caused by errors or omissions, whether such errors or omissions result from negligence, accident, or any other cause.

In order to maintain their anonymity, in some instances I have changed the names of individuals and places. I may have changed some identifying characteristics and

# CONTENTS.

behaviour patterns that you can learn - How to create a positive attitude - A real example of great attitude and persistence - A problem to solve is a resource for discovering your strengths. - Classification and Test on Character Strengths and Virtues. - HOW TO IDENTIFY YOUR WEAKNESSES. - HOW TO TAKE CONTROL OF YOUR WEAKNESSES. - DO YOU KNOW YOUR SKILLS? - DISCOVERING YOUR TALENTS.

**- THE SECOND STEP: WHAT DO YOU WANT?** THE WHEEL OF LIFE. - CREATE YOUR NEW LIFE WITH THE C.A.I.R.O. METHOD ® - THE CHARACTERISTICS OF A GOOD GOAL. - WHAT DOES S.M.A.R.T. MEAN? - Minimal Goal, Transitional Goals and Maximum Goal - WHICH IS YOUR FIRST IMPORTANT GOAL? -VISUALISE YOUR GOAL. - Write what you want to achieve in your life. - HOW CAN I SET MY GOAL? - FIND INSPIRATION FROM A TRUE STORY. - WHAT CAN BLOCK YOU ON THIS STEP?

**- THE THIRD STEP: WHY? - Why do you want to achieve your goal?** CLEAR VISION = CLEAR

MISSION. - CLEAR DECISION. - DISCOVERING THE MEANING BEHIND YOUR GOAL. - VALUES AND GOALS. - FIND YOUR MOTIVATIONS. - INTERNAL AND EXTERNAL MOTIVATORS. - The Question of your Destiny. - MY PERSONAL STATEMENT OF ACHIEVEMENT. - WHAT CAN BLOCK YOU ON THIS STEP?

- **THE FOURTH STEP: WHO?** Who is the protagonist of your story, your challenge and your dream? - Create good feeling with the people around you. - PAST VS. FUTURE. - CHANGE YOUR MINDSET. - THE FOUNDATION OF ACCEPTANCE - WHAT IS RESILIENCE? - How can resilience be developed or improved? - WHAT CAN BLOCK YOU ON THIS STEP?

- **THE FIFTH STEP: HOW?** HOW DO YOU THINK YOU WANT TO ACHIEVE YOUR GOAL? - THE WALT DISNEY MODEL. - What characterises a good action plan? - VISUALISE YOUR ACTION PLAN. - MAKE THE DIFFERENCE WITH BRAINSTORMING! - THE FOUR PS. - THE S.W.O.T. ANALYSIS. - ADVANTAGES AND

DISADVANTAGES. - IMPACT ACTION PLAN OR MASSIVE ACTION PLAN? - YOUR ACTION PLAN WITH THE EISENHOWER METHOD - WHAT CAN BLOCK YOU ON THIS STEP? - YOUR HABITS!

**- THE SIXTH STEP: IDENTIFY YOUR FACTORS OF SUCCESS!** - IDENTIFY YOUR FACTORS OF SUCCESS! - YOUR STRATEGIC RESULT AREAS. - WHAT CAN BLOCK YOU ON THIS STEP?

**- THE SEVENTH STEP: WHEN?** YOUR TIME AWARENESS. - DECIDE YOUR GOAL DEADLINE. - Break down your GOAL into STEPS! - YOUR ROAD MAP TO SUCCESS. - WHAT CAN BLOCK YOU ON THIS STEP?

**- THE EIGHTH STEP: WHERE?** WHERE DO YOU WANT TO ACHIEVE YOUR GOAL? - WHAT CAN BLOCK YOU ON THIS STEP?

**- THE NINTH STEP: THE POWER OF ACTION!** I WISH, I DREAM, I WANT, I REACH IT! - SUCCESS REQUIRES: Self-Awareness, Self-Discipline, Self-Control and Self-Mastery. - Self-mastery: how to become the master of your destiny.

4

*- THE SECRET TO ALWAYS BEING MOTIVATED.
- BE PROACTIVE: TAKE ACTION! - THE
POMODORO TECHNIQUE. - THE PARETO
PRINCIPLE. - C.A.R.S. Critical Analysis of Risks
and Success. © - A MODEL OF CRITICAL POINTS:
YOUR CRITICAL PATHWAY. - Monitor the threats
on your project. - WHAT CAN BLOCK YOU ON
THIS STEP?*

**- THE TENTH STEP: GIVE A PRIZE FOR YOUR
ACHIEVED GOALS! -** *The ability to replicate
success. - REFLECT ON YOUR SUCCESS. - THE
BENEFITS AND ADVANTAGES I GOT FROM MY
GOAL.*

**- EXTRA CONTENTS.** *Do you know what the
reasons for your procrastination are? - HOW YOU
CAN OVERCOME YOUR PROCRASTINATION -
SOME HELP TO REDUCE THE FEAR OF
SUCCESS. - A short story about me that I want
share with you.*

**Resources.**

**Sources and Bibliography.**

*'I dedicate this book to my sister Debora and to my family,*
*now far from me but close to my heart.'*

## *My special thanks to Roy Keene.*

*English Language Tuition in Kingston upon Thames.*

I acknowledge the great contribution of Mr. Roy Keene by his work correcting and enriching my chapters, and as my spoken English tutor.

Roy Keene is an English Language tutor living in South London near Kingston upon Thames. I chose Roy because he teaches in a friendly, relaxed atmosphere at his home.

Roy is qualified in Teaching English as a Foreign Language, and in teaching adults one-to-one; now he has about twenty years' experience and he also knows a lot about language and linguistics.

Roy is really passionate to his job; he has taught people of many nationalities. Roy can prepare you for exams such as FCE, IELTS or CAE if you wish. If you would like to improve your English, please contact Roy.

I hope to see you soon at Roy's lessons!

*http://www.roykeene.co.uk/*

## *My Acknowledgements.*

*With all my heart, I would like to thank all the people who have enabled me to write my first self-help book. I thank all those who gave me their support during the effort and joy of writing this useful manual for those who never stop dreaming.*

*The support of Cynthia who helped me to start my new life in England. The kindness of Josephine and Gary at Chessington Evangelical Church in giving me moments of joy despite their fight against her cancer.*

*The solidarity of Pauline, Julienne and Wendy at Brunswick Hub in giving me the opportunity to learn new things and regain confidence in myself during my residence in Leamington Spa, Warwickshire.*

*The continuous advice and supportive friendship from my Business Coach Jose Luis Ucar and his group of people at Finding Excellence, Kingston upon Thames, U.K. The constant support and inspiration of my Life Coach Laura and her group in Orpington, Kent, U.K.*

*To host families of my Au Pair program which was made possible by the tenacity of Miss Anna Ottone of the Welcome Agency in Turin, Italy.*

*To Sharon of the Ditton Business Centre and Mei-Mei who encouraged me to follow my dream to live in the U.K. during my darkest time.*

*To my colleagues and all staff at Hinchley Wood Secondary School in Esher, Surrey, that with their friendly and professional human environment I was made to feel part of a great team!*

*And finally, I wish to say thank you to Toastmasters International in Barking.*

***About me.***

*Dear reader, I am an Italian Life Coach and I began my studies with the Italian School of Life & Corporate Coaching founded by Luca Stanchieri, in Milan in 2015. I specialised in Corporate Coaching in Italy at the same school in that year. I presented my first public life coaching seminar in front of an audience of over fifty people, only two months after gaining my Life Coach Certificate, at the UIL (Unione Italiana Lavoratori, Italian Labour Union) headquarters in Alessandria, where I was a volunteer driver with the Trasporto Amico programme. I was a member of A.I.C.P. the Italian Association of Professional Coaches in 2016.*

*I challenged myself by cycling alone from Alessandria to the Principality of Monaco in 2016, in just two days, a real record if we think that I was overweight and had never made a long trip on a bicycle! During my stay in Warwickshire I walked hundreds of kilometres while visiting the county, but the purpose was to save on the high cost of bus fare!*

*In 2017 I volunteered for the Evolve Housing Plus charity both in Croydon and in Bromley, Kent. In 2018, I participated in a Performance Coaching programme with Grit (www.grit.org.uk) in collaboration with the Ark Academy of Wembley, a great experience that has allowed me to help young students achieve their goals, a memory that will stay forever in my heart, thanks above all to Sarah of GRIT. I continued my professional development with the Coaching Academy in the CPD (Continuing Professional Development) programme from 2018.*

*Introduction. How to use* The Ten Amazing Steps to Success!

*'If you want something, create it.'*

*Debora Cairo*

*The book 'The Ten Amazing Steps to Success!' was born from my need to create appropriate strategies for my goals, and I learned that there isn't a magic key to success in life and career, but as you know there are many paths that lead us to reach the desired goal and each one comes in its own way and in its own time.*

*It is important to recognise that it is possible to achieve results in life and this is the first premise to keep in mind, even when our goals aren't easy to accomplish. There are many factors that can help you to find those characteristics that are important to your life and career: initiative and self-confidence accompanied by genuine enthusiasm are always present in those who develop the ability to establish themselves in life, always being grateful to others around themselves.*

*With this book you can start a new experience that will allow you to know who you really are.* The Ten Amazing Steps to Success! *is organised in ten chapters that represent ten steps composed of original principles and lessons from humankind over the world. These steps belong to our history and have been used since ancient times to overcome limitations and barriers that our ancestors met during our evolution and civilisation; they are well known today and used in every human area such as economy, marketing, education, sport and personal development.*

*The Ten Steps can also be used in Life Coaching with numerous benefits for those who use them, creating enormous advantages in the main areas of life such as competence, relationships and autonomy.*

I decided to create a pathway through these steps as usually it isn't easy to find all of them put together in one manual. This pathway is based on the keys of success from successful people who used all the strategies, workouts and principles before us to achieve their goals, and now you will be inspired by the Ten Step, being driven to persevere into your dreams and goals.

This book with its numerous workouts and examples is a must-read for anyone wanting to transform each aspect of their life for the better. The Ten Amazing Steps to Success! offers the essential principles that you need if you want to become successful, have more fulfilling relationships and greater happiness.

Be sure to be focused during the reading so you can absorb every word and be ready to express your inner power.

**Remember**, it isn't possible to achieve your goals just by reading this book - you need to act because there are no results without action.

14

## IMPORTANT ADVICE.

To benefit from reading the book and the proposed workouts, I suggest to read a chapter every month or every two weeks. In this way you have time to think and do the exercises calmly, planning your projects and monitoring your progress.

**Remember** not to overdo it, respecting your life rhythms, your needs and the relations with other people around you.

**The Ten Steps follow an important principle: training theory.**

This book is oriented towards achieving goals and personal development through the continuous improvement of one's own performance, which can be an important pillar in achieving our happiness and self-realisation. At the same time thinking of improving only in terms of performance is harmful and useless.

Our happiness is based on other pillars such as love for oneself and others, enjoying life as a precious gift, managing one's own time effectively, finding time to devote to yourself and those in need, smiling at the beautiful things we come across every day, or crying when we need to, talking to a friend, and so on …

This book wants to help you achieve your success, but also give you the opportunity to reflect on what you really think is important in your life, trying to become aware of the person you are or want to be in spite of the difficulties you will encounter in your life path.

*Always ask yourself if it is worth bartering your true happiness for things that after a while lose their interest or are not for you.*

Now, I wish to show you a series of principles and rules of training theory as used in sporting disciplines which you can follow during your action plan. Among these that is particularly important is **the principle of loading**.

If you want to succeed in obtaining your best performance, you must know your current performance. For instance, it can be given by the number of pages that you can study in a certain number of hours a day for a week.

So, you need to clarify:
- the current performance that you have in the area you want improve.
- the new knowledge and skills that your new goal requires.

- a detailed plan for your future performances that will help you to achieve your goal.

It is important to understand that if you want to improve in any area you desire, the first phase is to consider accurately your current performances, which are the basis when you want to achieve a goal in life, sport or business; you need to know what your functional performance level is. At this stage you can observe and maintain your functional level over a week or two. (For example, you read five pages a day from your textbook, or twenty-five pages a week. Note how many hours this takes.)

Now it is possible to raise your functional level to an easily reachable goal, with an action plan of a week or a number of weeks, with low intensity practice and basic skills. (For instance, you can aim to study six pages a day or thirty pages in a week, and you can use the study skills that you already have.) In general, when you have achieved your new performance, you should reach a certain level of relaxation. In fact, if your goal becomes 'too easy' you will lose interest in it.

Once your new level is assured you can decide to increase your performance with a new target, and you can be ready for a new goal with a higher level of difficulty. (In our example, increasing the number of pages to thirty-five a week or a day will be your new goal. In this example, the increase is about 20% each time.) Often, an increase of 10% each time will be enough; you could be surprised, even getting a 100% increase over some weeks following this principle!

**Principle of individualised load**.
In this phase you need to identify your specific potential which you want to develop, or which strengths you want to improve according to your goal. And you have to target your progress at yourself as an individual. It is not about what other people or the average person can do. It is about what is right for you! In the science of sport, the principle of individualised load requires that training

stimuli be adapted to the psychophysical load capacity of the individual, to the ability to process them, and to the athlete's special needs; we can replicate this principle when we have to increase our skills and competency in any human sector. This principle can be applied in your life in various ways; in fact, you can personalise your tasks with different levels of execution during your action plan following your own vision, motivation, strengths and attitude. **Remember:** the individualised load reflects the principle that it is a process and you can increase your performances over a unit of time, recording your improvement step by step; an essential prerequisite for continuing to improve your performance is *to increase the load* by varying the difficulty of your tasks so that you can induce further changes with specific exercises for yourself.

The **variable load principle** and **principle of resting phases** are fundamental for your performance. In fact, loading and recovery must be planned together with an appropriate schedule because after increasing your performance there is a transient decrease in the ability to perform. One of the key factors for your performance is planning recovery processes that can help you, so be careful to plan your performances alternating with rest which allows your physical and mental energies to accumulate - especially if you are working under high pressure with a huge amount of stress. **Remember:** no work or performance can give improvement or increase without adequate rest. When you decide to increase your performance you must follow every single step explained above, making sure that your detailed performance plan matches your action plan and gives a significant contribution to it.

**How to use your logbook.**
In order to help you, I suggest you create your own personal **logbook** which can be based on a diary or a planner that you can tailor-make for yourself according to your needs. The logbook must report:

- your name and surname, the start date, the place from where you intend to realise your project.

- your project and how you want to do it; in addition, I suggest you write your personal diary every day, in the evening before going to sleep.

The workouts can be done in the book, but I recommend photocopying them (for personal use only) in order to have a clear trace of your journey towards the desired goal, later putting them in your logbook in chronological order. **Remember:** it is very important not to skip any steps as each step has its own importance and it is advisable to spend more time in taking advantage of the exercises thoroughly, and then act better, even if a bit later. It is also better to go to the next step only when you are sure you have given your best in the current step. Record your performances so you always have them at your fingertips at each stage.

'Two roads diverged in a yellow wood,

And sorry I could not travel both

And be one traveller long I stood

And looked down one as far as I could

To where it bent in the undergrowth;

Then took the other, as just as fair,

And having perhaps the better claim,

Because it was grassy and wanted wear;

Though as for that the passing there

Had worn them really about the same,

And both that morning equally lay

In leaves no step had trodden black.

Oh, I kept the first for another day!

Yet knowing how way leads on to way,

*I doubted if I should ever come back.*

*I shall be telling this with a sigh*

*Somewhere ages and ages hence:*

*Two roads diverged in a wood, and I*

*I took the one less travelled by, And that has made*
*all the difference.'*

*Robert Frost*

## FIRST STEP

READY TO DISCOVER YOURSELF?

Are you able to sacrifice what you are for what you want to become?

Why did you see a white sheet just now?

Because from a white sheet…

You will be able to write

a  new  chapter  of your life!

I am sure that you have met a lot of people around you who can easily make a list of their limitations in achieving the life they desire; their list could contain at least ten negative thoughts that support their thesis, that it isn't easy or possible to achieve their goals, or yours.

You will be surprised by 126 suggestions and pieces of advice by **Napoleon Hill**. They still sound modern nowadays. This advice is stronger than the negative attitudes and complaints people often have, and you could be inspired by them to create a new mindset.

Are you able to reconsider your own mind limits in a different way?

**Workout 1** **Date:**

I've chose some of the Napoleon Hill's 126 pieces of advice to invite you to evaluate how they could help you. Tick those sentences that you want to learn and describe in your diary or Logbook and what they mean to you.

- Stop whining. Learn from your mistakes.

- Fear less and Be invincible, so plan to be successful.

- Let yourself be inspired.

- Be more efficient with your time. Decide to take action today.

- Fight against mediocrity.

- Compliment with others' ideas.

- Work on being patient and stay in mental shape.

- Shake hands while looking at the other person's eyes.

- Give an opinion when it is hard.

- Care about others, sharing more and donate time to charity.

- Pay attention to details.

- Love someone.

- Have a dream and write down your thoughts.

- Apologise more and pay attention to the conversation.

- Have a purpose every day. Don't stop until you finish.

- Appreciate differences and decide to learn from everyone.

- Be less selfish and smile at those around you.

- Imagine the possibilities.

- Fail gracefully. Decide to be optimistic.

- Ask more questions and ask for help.

- Read a new biography.

- Do something outrageous. Explore new ideas.

- Be more effective with your talents. Feed your inspiration.

- Pursue your goals each day. Make a list of tasks to get done.

- Live with honour.

- Work on your biggest weakness.

- Meditate on your goals. Do good things for the right reasons.

- Let life happen around you.

   Decide that caring is more important than winning.

# WHAT DOES SUCCES MEAN?

I would like to share with you the meaning of the term success. Are you aware of its true meaning?

*Understanding the meaning of success is one of the most important pillars for people like you who want to accomplish goals.*

Try to describe your opinion based both on your life experience and on what you know about success so you can compare it with the description I have written for you on the following pages.

**Workout 2**                                    **Date:**

In my opinion, success means:

What people around me think about success:

Your ideas and beliefs about success are based on your life experiences and the opinions of others, as well as the type of education received from your family, school and social influences in your environment.

Is it important to know the meaning of the term success? The answer is yes! My explanation will guide you to its deepest meaning: often we are surrounded by examples of successful people, who through their abilities or profession have achieved fame or remarkable results in life.

Often success is linked to dreams of being rich and famous, owning dream cars and living in an immense house and being in wonderful places. Well, when luck is out of the way I can say that most of the people who achieve success in their life have made great efforts and sacrifices.

Is success just a life of money and beautiful houses like the mass media and the social networks show us every day? I do not believe so. Success, when it is pure and genuine, is very often made from enormous sacrifices and inner struggles, struggles that sometimes lead to disappointment. But our success and happiness can also be the best revenge, as well as having a great positive pride in overcoming great challenges!

Does success only mean challenges and sacrifices?

Think about these realities; for instance: sudden rain, a dog escaped from its owner, a child who is born and makes his family happy, a river that overflows and invades cities and countries. What are these facts?

These are events that happen in reality; events that have different origins, their own natures and causes. When these events happen, they modify the order of nature at a certain point in time.

This 'power' to change things is possessed by nature and its creatures and by human beings, who can consciously choose to change the reality which they live in according to their thoughts and actions. From this definition I am pleased to tell you that every event that happens has its origin and its end.

In practice, every time you think and act you have the power to change your reality.

Using the same power, you can repeat this indefinitely. In fact, *various complete actions create a process that has its origin in your imagination.*

| SUCCESS | A PROCESS |
|:---:|:---:|
| = | = |
| PROCESS | COMPLETED STEPS |

**Remember:** *success is the ability to make things happen through a process made of completed steps in reality.*

*You are also able to carry out a process that leads you to success!*

*Now, knowing the real meaning of the term success, you know that every time you do a series of actions, you demonstrate your ability to carry out a process, which could be linked to your will to succeed.*

Some examples can clarify this concept about the ability to make things happen:

- when you leave the house and close the door behind you.

- when you decide to read a book.

- when you make a phone call to a distant relative.

- when you are preparing for an important exam.

- when you run a marathon.

- when you are doing the shopping.

As you have just seen in these examples, it is easy to understand that each time you act you create a process that changes your reality, making new events happen.

*It is important to understand that our actions, while having a different nature, are merely just actions. It is the meaning we give to our actions and above all the results obtained that make us able to say if we have succeeded.*

*Success must be in line with our expectations which vary from person to person. So, we must learn to see success with different eyes; we can see it as a series of events that happen over time and in reality without judging them.*

Look at the definition taken from a business site:

1. Achievement of an action within a specified period of time. Success can also mean completing an objective or reaching a goal. Success can be expanded to encompass an entire project or be restricted to a single component of a project or task. It can be achieved within the workplace, or in an individual's personal life.

2. Colloquial term used to describe a person that has achieved his or her personal, financial or career goals.

Now you have understood that you have the possibility and the power to create your own life, challenging yourself with sacrifices in accordance with your goals and personal desires and needs.

If you want succeed it is important to understand what success means to you, rather than being influenced by its superficial meaning. *Because success is the value that you give to your actions.*

**Workout 3**                                             **Date:**

Now, re-evaluate what success means to you with these questions:

What is important to you now and in the future?

How do you think you can create the life you want?

## SUCCESS IS AN ICEBERG

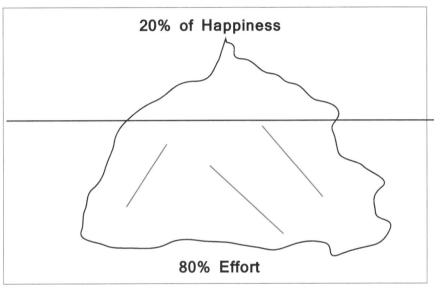

**20% of Happiness**

**80% Effort**

Success is the result of many actions that over a period of time make something happen in reality; in accordance with this explanation, everyone can reach success with different results related to their personal expectations and connected to their values and beliefs.

Are you ready to make the effort that make up 80% of success to reap 20% of happiness?

43

It seems a small percentage but we can't measure our emotions with numbers or statistics. Many people would like to buy their happiness if they could have the opportunity, but not everyone is prepared to make the effort to accomplish their desires. It is important to be satisfied and feel happy as we are taking the road to success and developing our personal empowerment before our pure goals.

What does it mean to make 80% effort?

It means that if you want to change something important in your life or achieve your personal goal you need to being focused and committed for a period of time, and this is the pillar of your success and happiness. Maybe at this moment you don't have the right attitudes, but you can learn them during your action plan and keep in mind that they are useful to your existence and not only to your project.

**Remember:** the most important thing is *your satisfaction* during your journey to your next goal.

When you want to change your life or achieve your burning desire, it is important to keep in mind the importance of your path to success and your own decisions. To choose and to decide are the most important steps before starting to plan any goals in your life. But your decision, believe me, isn't enough.

*First you need to choose what you want to do and then decide firmly that you will get on with it.*

Do you want to stay in your comfort zone forever or do you prefer to find new scope in your life? Do you feel happy to do the same things every day, or do you want to challenge yourself by starting something new and amazing?

*Whatever your decision is you will have decided anyway. There are no right or wrong decisions but only decisions, different decisions that lead to different results.*

**Are you able to sacrifice yourself for what you want to become?**

Ask yourself: do I want to stay where I am now or do I want to go where I really want to be, discovering who I am? What can I do in the future?

Through the pages of this book you will understand how to walk on the path to success seeing yourself in a different way that you would never have thought possible.

Be ready to discover new ideas, new skills and new exciting relationships.

**In what areas of my life do I want to improve or feel in crisis?**

Many times you have desired to find answers to these questions in your life, and through the following pages you will discover that a single area in your life, if improved or changed, can make the difference. So, being accomplished and happy is not impossible.

Sometimes you can feel sad or euphoric like on a swing, your mood has highs and lows and this confuses you, and you don't understand why. Well, with the workouts in this book you can realise that it is possible to change your mind about situations and yourself. Little by little and with the right attitude you will get the benefits and then see profound changes in yourself.

*Discovering who you are, what your true nature is and your potential are the first steps in building your happiness.* This is the most important thing to accomplish in our lives, and in my opinion it shouldn't be confused with selfishness.

A life purpose, or a goal, is your opportunity to assess yourself and understand who you are, as well as what you want to get from your life.

*The first thing in our life, alongside a goal, is to achieve happiness.*

In the next exercise you will be able to evaluate the following areas: **Competence, Relationships and Autonomy**.

As the *Self-Determination Theory* elaborated by **Deci and Ryan** explains, we have to develop and satisfy three main areas in our lives to make us feel fulfilled and happy as human beings. This perfect situation rarely occurs in reality, nevertheless some of us are able to create fulfilling lives and existences.

Successful people who have a balanced life at the same time can accomplish their goals in the three areas mentioned above.

How do they do that? They simply develop the right mindset and thanks to personal experience gained in the three areas they give importance only to the things that they really care about.

### Competence.

As **Luca Stanchieri**, the founder of the Scuola Italiana Life & Corporate Coaching, has explained, Competence is the need to feel integrated in harmony with the environment and the contexts in which we live.

*Happiness in this area is based on your activities and being motivated to excel. In this area you can estimate how much your skills can influence your professional achievement.*

By giving a value to this area, you will realise if you have any gaps in your profession for instance. Not only that, you can also 'measure' if your skills meet your current criteria based on your professional experience; for example: am I able to use the latest software in my projects as my company requires? Can I teach following current school updates? Can I be an assertive leader? And again, am I prepared to complete all my studies?

The questions you ask yourself can help you to stay on the pathway that you will choose towards your goal, changing or improving some aspects at any time. Keep in mind that if you are lacking in any competences you can always learn and improve over time and ask for advice from experts.

If you want to develop new skills and competences, always prepare to reach a higher level and make a difference in your job. The Competence areas can be related to career, organisation skills, social and communication skills, increasing in performances, maximising your abilities and strengths, sense of purpose, goal setting, productivity and taking action, money and finance.

## Relationships.

This area reveals your desire to belong to a group of people and to feel loved and considered as an individual.

In this area you can feel motivated to love the people around you making new relationships, but at the same time it could reveal unhealthy ways of relating to other people or a need to stay in toxic relationships, manipulating others or being manipulated.

Our relationships are important in our lives, especially when we want to live happily together with others. If this does not happen we enter a spiral of sadness, depression, anger and melancholy. Fortunately, it isn't always like this.

In our life nothing can be done without human relations; even when you drive your car, it wouldn't exist without the work of those who designed and built it. Or think for instance, if you were a child without your parents' support and education, you could not have learned anything - such as how to talk! And how can we forget our first teacher who taught us how to write? We should always be grateful to the people around us and adopt an open mind towards other cultures, respecting our culture first.

At the same time human relationships are not always the way we want them to be; in fact we can have problems in the family, with friends and colleagues or with our boss.

*Our relationships are based on our expectations.*

For example, if somebody doesn't act as you would desire you can be disappointed and upset by him or her. In our relationships it is important to understand how to handle certain situations and the possible misunderstandings. The wish to improve your relationships can be fulfilled by doing a self-analysis and then acting in accordance to new insight. You must also think about relationships in your profession or future work. In fact, nowadays it is important to create good human relations at the workplace. Think how many people are dissatisfied with colleagues or their bosses! Working side by side with people that we do not like is stressful, and this also causes problems with health and low job satisfaction. At the same time if you are self-employed you need to learn how to manage your clients' moods and your business partnerships with other experts, both professionally and in a human sense.

It is also important to understand that if we have gaps in our human relationships, both at work and with family and friends, maybe the time has come to look inside ourselves and boldly understand how to improve ourselves to change our personal attitudes to the people around us.

In workout number 4 you will evaluate how you react in your relationships and especially if you are happy with the people around you.

If we assign a low score, from 1 to 5, it is important not to blame ourselves. We should evaluate different situations in a detached and objective way so as to be clear about what is happening.

Learn and evaluate if you are still in your comfort zone and protecting yourself rather than creating new human relationships.

The Relationship areas that you could consider improving are:
- dating and relationships
- social/communication skills
- work/life balance

## Autonomy

According to Luca Stanchieri, Autonomy reflects the sense of self that nurtures one's self-determination, regulating itself from time to time and finding an expression outside of external control, becoming aware of our ideas, passions and goals in life.

This process can generate conflicts as happens in young people who embody the spirit of freedom and the desire to be independent of the bonds of their childhood.

In this area the desire to be motivated at every level of our lives is strong. I can say that Autonomy is connected with the need to be free and to be yourself. Are you really aware of making your choices in a free and independent way? Think for a moment how much pressure we suffer every day from the mass media!

Even in our family or between friends, we can be affected by the persuasive charm of their ideas or by the suggestions of others. And up to here everything is fine.

Then you will do as you want, won't you? This happens because you think and act as an adult person, aware of your value, giving you the freedom to express your needs, desires and opinions. And when this does not happen? When was the last time you thought you had done the wrong thing just to satisfy other people? Do you feel serene and happy with your decision? Have courage and tell yourself the truth!

*Being autonomous is another important pillar in achieving a fulfilling and happy life. Analysing and understanding where we fail to be completely 'free' to think and act must be our top priority, especially when we decide to take the path to success.*

How can you be free to decide if you can't distinguish your own decisions from those made for you by someone else? Being independent also means being aware of your skills and abilities. Only a person aware of this can feel independent to choose and decide, both in life and at work. Think of illiterate people who will never be able to decide their future serenely. Image if you were an entrepreneur who always has to pay experts because you don't know enough about your job or project. You would not be free to choose independently and look for the best strategy for your business!

Your skills and your relationships are important to help you to become more autonomous, but above all your love for yourself, when it is positive and not self-centred, can help you most.

Search for people with whom you can open up to and have new experiences and step by step you will gain greater awareness of yourself. Moreover, by becoming master of your reactions, you can also change the way you see yourself and the world around you.

The Autonomy areas that can help you to get more confident and take control of your life are:
- self-confidence and self-love
- self-belief and self-development
- overcoming comfort zone and procrastination
- negative habits and finding motivation
- time management
- health/well-being and stress management

**Workout 4**                                               **Date:**

Assign a value from 1 to 10 to each area represented. We have marked the area of Competence with C, the area of Autonomy with A and the area of Relationships with R.

Then describe what you want to improve in the respective areas of your life.

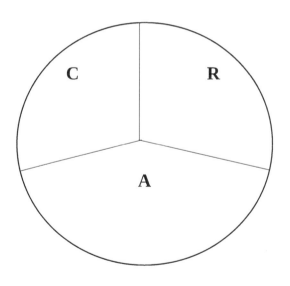

Competence:

Relationships:

Autonomy:

Values from 1 to 5, are low values that can give two different types of result. If you say for example: 'I don't have any friends,' it could be a lack of confidence in the relationships area, while if you say 'I don't want to have friendships,' it can be that you don't have any trouble in being alone and therefore it isn't a problem for you.

If, instead, having friends is your goal but you aren't able to build new relationships, here the low score shows that you have gaps in the relationships area, so the low score should be seen in a negative way.

*It is important to understand that whatever value you give to an area does not mean having to accept the situation forever.* The purpose of this workout is to understand where to start improving and to realise that it is possible.

Scores from 6 to 10 usually demonstrate good balance within the areas shown. Sometimes the values can satisfy your criteria, while if you try to improve yourself, the value you have given will give you a starting point and a point for your improvement.

Having similar scores in all areas demonstrate balance for scores from 6 to 10, while low values denote disequilibrium.

- My best areas are:

- The areas that I want to improve are:

# YOUR BELIEF SYSTEM

*' A map is not the territory'*

*A. Korzybski.*

The way that you interpret the reality around you determines your feelings. Pay attention to how you see the world; always remember that you will interpret the world according to your view of it. You will experience emotions at first and then feelings, which will create your thoughts from which your future actions will be born.

Think for a moment about how you respond to others' words, intentions, actions and reactions, because how you think can make the difference in your life and your relationships.

If you believe that where you are living it is impossible to find a job that is suitable for you, then you won't find any jobs. Again, if you believe that you aren't able to improve your skills it will be very hard to develop or learn something new.

*Your beliefs can limit your life, and a good way to stop this happening is to identify the beliefs that are limiting you.*

'A map isn't the territory' means that what you think or believe is not reflected in reality until you are able to match your beliefs with the evidence around you.

The following workout can help you to analyse what your beliefs are and how to modify them positively.

(Write down your answers in your logbook and check them after three months to see if you have changed your beliefs.)

**Remember:** *beliefs aren't good or bad, but it is their impact on your life that can determine whether or not you accomplish your vision and goals.*

**Workout 5**                                                **Date:**

1) Start identifying your past beliefs and then your current beliefs. Pay attention to which ones could block you.

2) Explore the origins of your beliefs and the reasons why you are continuing to follow them.

3) Look at the evidence: sometimes your beliefs are supported by a 'false perception of reality'. You need to find proof that your beliefs are true and realistic.

4) Take action: compare your new evidence with your old beliefs and create new behaviour patterns that can permit you to change your mindset. Always consider options that you have never considered before.

5) Previously, how convinced were you of reaching your goal? And how convinced are you that it is possible now?

# YOUR THINKING PATTERNS.

*When you learn how to recognise your beliefs and their impact on your life you can manage them, being aware of the thinking patterns that can limit or liberate you.*

Transforming your old thinking patterns into positive thinking will allow you to consider doing something new that puts you outside of your comfort zone, because if you think you can't then you won't. If you think you can then you will.

**Remember**: you are what you think, and you will become what you think.

This is one the most influential mottos of many famous people in history from Gautama Siddharta, Albert Einstein and Zig Ziglar, to authors and speakers such as Tony Robbins or Adele Basheere who has written this motto in her company greeting cards! It's the idea of believing that you can achieve your values and goals.

*Believe within yourself that you are worthy of success and that you can gain it.*

In the next workout record the negative thought patterns that you have. And on the following page imagine the positive thoughts that can replace them.

---

**Workout 6**                                    **Date:**

### The thinking patterns that can limit me:

E.g: 'I am stupid... I am unlucky... I am ugly... I am too old...

---

**Workout 7**                                        **Date:**

### The thinking patterns that can liberate me.

E.g: 'I am not ugly. In fact I can't please everybody, but maybe I can take care of myself by improving my style and learning how to present myself to others better.'

# WHAT IS YOUR BIGGEST LIMITATION?

*Resolve say, I will. The man says, 'I will climb this mountain. They told me it is too high, too far, too steep, too rocky and too difficult. But it is my mountain. I will climb it and you will soon see me waving from the top or dead on the side from trying.'* Jim Rohn

---

**Workout 8**                                    **Date:**

Describe your biggest limitation which is blocking your way towards personal fulfilment and how you plan to overcome it.

My biggest limitation is:

---

And it is in the following area:

Competence ☐     Relationships ☐     Autonomy ☐

How I want to overcome my biggest limitation:

## MIND YOUR LIMITS.

*'Your current limitations or failures are the building blocks from which to create greatness. You can go where you want to go. You can do what you want to do. You can become what you want to become. You can do it all, starting now, right where you are.'*        *Jim Rohn*

Our society and culture give us a false teaching about our limits. In fact, we see them as barriers in front us and it is hard to see the opportunities behind the limits that we meet every day.

*Don't see your limitation as a limit but see it as a challenge.*

We have grown up with certain kinds of limits that originated in our childhood, teenage and adult age, and we have to evaluate why and how these limits could block us at the present time.

Are you free and able to choose and decide which are the limitations that you can overcome in your life?

Think deeply on this question because it is a good opportunity to understand the difference between the limits that you have inside of yourself and the limitations that your environment gives you, and how you could be influenced by these two kinds of limits.

Think how your life could be different without certain limits imposed by society or the expectation of our culture. Many people around you are unhappy and confused about their own life because they aren't living the life they really want; they are following the limitations imposed on them or their old limiting habits instead of their desires or goals. They are thinking that they are not to be allowed to be happy.

Again, think how different your life can be if you can change your current situation little by little, improving yourself through new experiences and new friendships, and at the same time discovering the real meaning behind your limitations by transforming old habits into winning actions which help you to create a new belief system about yourself.

You can identify four areas, where it is easier to recognise your limits: the limits of your body, the limits of your thoughts, the technological equipment limits you have and finally the limits you find in the environment around you.

## Don't allow your limits to block you!

When you have positive criteria in a certain area it is good training to use your best qualities and skills to support the areas that are weak or you want improve.

For instance, if your financial situation is satisfactory and you don't have to make great efforts or sacrifices, you could take seminars or courses that can help you to learn new skills, like learning a new language or a software programme. Another idea is to offer one or more of your competencies to help other people around you, which is a good opportunity to find a new relationship!

## Body Limits.

When are we in the presence of body limits? When we become aware that our body cannot carry out some activities in our life, such as certain types of sports or work.

It may also happen that we have a body outside the common standards (always imposed by the society in which we live and by the mass media). For some people at every terrestrial latitude, being shorter, taller, fatter, thinner, too smart or too beautiful can be torture.

Being different from others may be seen as a disadvantage in this world, but if you are able to look deeply into yourself you can discover your unique inner power. I prefer to see the word 'too' in a different way, I wish to give it a positive meaning. For me it means more.

*Yes, you have more rather than less, because you are with qualities and skills that not everyone around you has!*

---

**Workout 9**                                    **Date:**

I am too... (I have more rather than less):

---

Sometimes I think how my life could be different if I was tall rather than short. I remember when at secondary school somebody said to me: 'Cristian, you are too small to ride a motorbike, for you it will be only a dream.'

Well, my dear friend, from that day at school I started to do the impossible to overcome my limitations. Nobody knows how much effort I made but I am sure of this: I am ready to repeat every moment that has allowed me to become the person who I am.

Do you know that I am a proud motorbiker who rides his old Ducati Monster?

So, after many years, I'm grateful to the classmate who pushed me to improve myself - although he was hateful and stupid.

We know the fatigue of living with a body that it isn't perfect or that shows disabilities, but at the same time I know that people with these conditions are the best people in the world; they are examples for us, they show us how it is possible to transform certain body conditions into big opportunities, and how we can have an amazing life - *choosing to be happy!*

*Choose to be happy: it is possible when you accept yourself and your body limits as a way of transforming your entire existence, looking at the options instead of the limits that nature has imposed on you.*                    *Cristian Cairo*


I wish to tell you something amazing about two people who have inspired me. One is the fantastic Italian girl Beatrice Maria Vio, or, as people know her, 'Bebe', and the other is the clever Nick Vujicic, the famous Australian evangelist and inspirational speaker.

Bebe is a wonderful Italian wheelchair fencer who was the European Champion in 2014 and 2016, World Champion in 2015 and 2017, and Paralympic Champion in her category in 2016. She fell ill with severe meningitis that caused a dangerous necrosis resulting in amputation of both her legs and her forearms. Rehabilitation and her love of fencing have allowed Bebe to come back and practise her favourite sport. She is a champion wheelchair fencer who can hold the foil using prosthetics, fencing from her shoulder.

Bebe is an inspirational young woman. In fact, with her parents she founded the non-profit organisation Art4Sport Onlus, with which Bebe is promoting sport for young amputees. At the Milan Expo in 2015 she was the ambassador for Milan City, and she published her first autobiography, *Mi hanno regalato un sogno (They gave me a dream)*. As a consequence of her hard experience she has become a campaigner for early vaccination.

I find it interesting to listen to Nick Vujicic. In fact he is one of my favourite speakers in the world! Let's start with his early life. Nicholas James Vujicic born with the tetra-amelia syndrome, a disorder that is characterised by the absence of arms and legs. Initially, his parents didn't want him, but fortunately they understood that it was God's plan for Nicky. He was born with both feet deformed having the toes fused to the feet. Later an operation allowed to Nicky to use his toes like fingers to hold things or to turn pages for instance. The amazing outcome is that he is able to drive his electric wheelchair and use his laptop and mobile phone.

Nicky knew the meaning of being bullied in his life and as a consequence he tried to commit suicide. Fortunately, later on his mother began to believe in him and they started to speak about other disabilities in their prayer group. With support from both his family and his church Nicky was able to graduate at twenty-one with a Bachelor of Commerce degree, showing himself what his real inner power was.

He is married to a fantastic woman, Kanae Miyahara, who met him during a public meeting. The couple are proud of their four children.

In 2005 he founded **Life Without Limbs**, an organisation that helps people with disability all over the world, but that isn't all. Nicky Vujicic was an actor in a short movie and he has recorded a single called 'Something More'. Nicky has written over ten books that motivate people to overcome their limits and fears.

With these two examples I wanted to give you the opportunity to think in a different way about your own body limits and especially the limits that can block you from realising your happiness, the limits that have their origins in your thoughts.

## Thought Limits.

*Know yourself, be your master. Your mind can make the difference in your life: as you think you act.*

Your past experiences, your background, your education and your beliefs and values drive you every day. Try to imagine if you thought you wouldn't be able to reach your goals in life. Maybe you would not be the same person that you are today. Your choices are shaped by your values and beliefs. What happens when there isn't a symbiosis between your life goals and your values? You can lose your life balance and this happens because you don't act as yourself.

Do you remember when I told you about the areas of competence, relationships and autonomy? Well, these are the areas most connected with your thoughts and your thoughts can influence your life positively or negatively. If you are not free to think in autonomy from internal/external influences, you will always be in doubt about yourself and uncertain about how to act.

When you want to achieve your goals you have to see yourself as a marathon runner or as a body builder. Your body may not be prepared (body limit) but with your tenacity and your inner strength you can overcome yourself in transforming your body and your mind, to be like a marathon runner or body builder.

Keep your mind under control and measure your performance regularly; try to understand how you can overcome your mind limits but be respectful to yourself, because the best way to change your mind limits is to practise step by step!

# The Technical Equipment Limits.

As the title suggests the technical equipment limits appears when our technical preparation or technical equipment can't meet the requirements that our goal or project needs. Maybe we have basic equipment such as obsolete technical instruments.

For instance, you need to buy a new mobile phone with the Android system because you have to use WhatsApp to call your friends, or you have to change your equipment if it is broken or inadequate. Try to imagine your next trip to Amazonia without a GPS, a modern off-road car or medicines against dangerous insect bites!

Technical equipment limits are what we call any parts of your equipment that don't allow you to proceed without disturbance or delay, while technical limits are connected to your own preparation and your skills.

## Environmental Limits.

Can our environment make a difference in our lives? In part we can say yes, but it isn't fundamental. Let's me tell you why.

As Environment Limits we mean the limits that you can find in your environment and your environment is made by: your family, your friends, your schools and education, your job and colleagues, your spare time activities or hobbies, and the places where you have lived and you are living. Our environment is important because it can give us the resources that we need to develop as a child and as an adult in a balanced way.

For example, you may or may not get an appropriate education at school, or you can or can't find the right people that you deserve for your personal development.

If you can't find a behavioural model in your childhood, maybe as an adult you will have certain problems with your self-esteem or in your relationships.

Then again, if you are an entrepreneur you will need to find the right equipment or the experts who can give advice on your projects and sometimes it isn't easy to find these resources near to your workplace or business place.

The environment can permit to you to survive. Think for a moment if you were born in a poor country without any health care, or in a dangerous neighbourhood surrounded by gangs and weapons.

Fortunately, as human beings and individuals, we can solve and overcome these kinds of environmental problems; the best way is to start to analyse what is happening around us. The next step is to accept it. Accepting problems as challenges and not as limits imposed by the environment in which we live has allowed us as humans to survive and realise our current technological development with enormous sacrifices and revolutionary ideas.

All this happened because some human beings decided to challenge their fears about nature and the world around them. They transformed their limitations into great opportunities that marked the birth of mankind as we know it today.

*What makes the difference in your environment is you.*

In the next workout you will evaluate how to face your main four limits, successfully overcoming them and growing as a person at the same time!

**Workout 10**                                    *Date:*

*Use the main areas Competence, Relationships and Autonomy to identify your limitations so it will be easy to check and control them. (In Autonomy you could have all four kind of limits, while in Competence you can find Technical Equipment limits and in the Relationship area you could have Thought and Environment limits.)*

- Find out how your body could block you, and find in yourself the resources to overcome your body limits:

- Think about your Thought Limits and start to manage your self-beliefs in a different way; allow yourself to find the right mindset for your goal and action plan:

- Monitor the Technical Equipment aspects of your goal, evaluate your equipment and find options that can allow to you to solve the problems you will meet.

- Consider which limits in your environment can block you. Try to set up a different solution that helps you to overcome or circumnavigate these limits:

# THE BARRIERS TO YOUR SUCCESS.

I remember with nostalgia when my uncle Pietro told me about the figure of Giuseppe Borsalino, the founder of the oldest luxury hat factory in Italy. Borsalino inspired me because he had courage and persistence that allowed his factory to become world famous. Since 1857 Borsalino's factory has been based in Alessandria, Piedmont.

Before the First World War, Borsalino made more than two milion hats per year and he hired over 2500 employees, becoming a great resource for the little town where the Company was located.

Borsalino fought against a very adverse rural environment when he set up his business; but by his determination he converted Alessandria into a modern town with many aqueducts, hospitals, a sanatorium and a retirement home. Borsalino was a forward-thinking man for his time. In fact he always supported his employees with modernisation, a company welfare programme and a pension.

Borsalino is still an example for us. He reveals that anything is possible and we can follow his story and be inspired by his fierce humanity; through his efforts Giuseppe Borsalino overcame those barriers that could block him from becoming successful in his field... of felt hats. His amazing hats were appreciated by Hollywood stars. In fact his products were well known in the U.K. and U.S.

In the next chapter you will understand how your barriers can block your desire to accomplish your goal.

*Maybe in your life you saw the barriers and limits around you as something impossible to overcome, change or solve, because you saw them just as barriers.*

Are successful people able to overcome every barrier they met during their journey on the road of success? Maybe not. The barriers they met were turned into opportunities because they wanted to discover new approaches and create new options that could help them to solve their problems. Many people around you have transformed their limits and barriers into opportunities that gave them the possibilities they needed.

If you know *the nature of your biggest barrier,* it will be possible for you to change your life completely. Accept the fact that your barriers can block your personal goal.

*You will see two roads ahead. One is a new road of change and the other one is the road of your past. You won't know what is the best road for you. Anyway, whatever road you choose it will be your own responsibility, even if you decide to stay on the road of your past.*

The solution to your barriers will be on the new road, but you won't know that until you get to your destination, following your decision and your own destiny to the end.

It is important not to stay focused on your barriers and see them just as barriers but to try to discover how to overcome or circumnavigate them. Are you ready for that?

**Workout 11**                                    **Date:**

- Describe the origin and the nature of your current barriers:

**Workout 12**                                    **Date:**

Some barriers can be overcome by your strength, your effort, your determination. But some barriers - you have to find a way to go around them, which may require some patience rather than force.

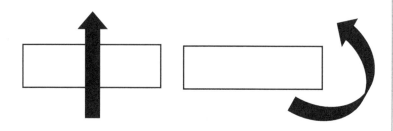

- Think how it is possible to overcome your barriers successfully:

- Think how you can circumnavigate those barriers that can block you. By creating new approaches and options, you can go around them.

- Think what else could block your project:

## HOW TO RECOGNISE THE IMPOSTOR SYNDROME.

Do women or men suffer more from Impostor Syndrome? Until recent years research had studied this problem among career women, and it was erroneously thought that it mainly concerned women. Nowadays it appears that both women and men suffer from it, but they talk about it and deal with it in different ways.

It often happens that we consider the people around us as more capable than ourselves of achieving goals and therefore capable of enjoying success while we do not do the same for ourselves. We do not consider ourselves deserving either of achieving results or of arriving at the longed for success. Indeed, we give the unsatisfactory explanation that what we do achieve is because of luck or that we have obtained it without merit. We feel like impostors if we achieve success in life and create the habit of masking our inadequacy if we do not achieve it, and if we do obtain results we tend to hide ourselves for fear of making mistakes that could jeopardise our credibility as successful and capable people in order to achieve results in life.

One of the characteristics of Impostor Syndrome is confronting others, sometimes blaming them for unachieved successes. We must learn not to fall into the trap of confrontation with others, for when we are dealing with ourselves we can only see our imperfections, while judgement towards others is based on impressions that often do not represent reality. Usually we tend to make positive judgements about others without knowing them deeply.

Are you thinking that you are affected by Impostor Syndrome too? I would like to give you some practical advice to overcome this kind of negative thought for your well-being and personal fulfilment.

In fact, thinking we are inadequate is a negative thought pattern that our brain carries out with the aim of avoiding suffering, to protect us from dangers whether they are real or not, but unfortunately the result is to create limiting beliefs that do not allow us to express our strengths.

**How to take control of the Impostor Syndrome.**

When you feel inadequate or ashamed write it down immediately in your diary or logbook. Make a list of all the ways in which this trap manifests itself. For example, if you are doing something but think you are failing and feeling inadequate. What are the situations in which you feel insecure? When do you not feel on top of the situation? When do you think people lose trust in you?

Analysing the most varied situations in which you feel this way can be a valuable help to make you more aware; understand that you can solve this by finding solutions and strategies useful to overcoming these thoughts. Resist the temptation to stay in your comfort zone and try not to run away from your Impostor Syndrome, but calmly, and with conviction, face your sense of inadequacy because only then can you defeat it. I did this and my life has improved a lot giving me much personal satisfaction.

## Evaluate your thoughts.

Evaluate your thoughts against the evidence. You have to consider what is true or false. Think for a moment if there is a real connection between your personal beliefs and reality and try not to judge yourself too severely. Rather, try to understand what is really stopping your achievements.

So, make a list of your strengths and weaknesses. You could do it alone or with people you trust who must give you their feedback.

Also, do the same workout with the same people; make a list of their strengths and weaknesses and give your feedback on which areas could improve. Compare these lists with those you have done for yourself as you will notice you are much more lenient with the people around you. Keep in mind that this workout helps you to see yourself in a more balanced way.

**Workout 13**                                             **Date:**

Evaluate     your     Impostor     Syndrome's     limiting
thoughts.

Now, make a short list of your strengths and weaknesses.

**Workout 14**                                          **Date:**

Evaluate your thoughts about yourself as compared with your view of other people and their view of you.

**Create connections with people in your community.**

In the previous workout you discovered that the people around you also have qualities and weaknesses. You can benefit from opening up with others and helping them to talk about themselves at the same time. In this way you feel useful and you can learn to manage your choices better - they must be based on the important concept of your own worth and you can compare yourself with people without losing your dignity, but rather you will contribute positively to a positive human environment.

**Workout 15**                                    **Date:**

Write here how you would like to start improving your attitude towards people. Make a weekly plan for every sort of activity that can help you to make progress in your current relationships, and check your progress at the end of the month:

## Learn to receive compliments

When someone gives you a compliment do not immediately find an excuse to say that you don't deserve it. Simply be happy and reply 'thank you'; write down the compliments you received so you have a way to encourage yourself in your darkest moments. Keep them as a record to help you improve.

**Remember:** successes will be composed of both your efforts and luck, which even if it contributes to your success does so in a small percentage.

Be realistic and quantify the impact of good fortune and your own hard work that have enabled you to achieve your success.

**Write down your strategies for fighting Impostor Syndrome.**

Once you have identified the mind traps which you fall into most often, try to write sentences that make you regain confidence instead. Always keep them with you so you can read them whenever you need to and because they will help you remember how much you're worth.

It can help you recall your past success, big or small, leaving you with the positive feelings that these memories have aroused.

**Workout 16**                                          **Date:**

My motivating sentences:

1-

2-

3-

4-

5-

## An optimist's special behaviour patterns that you can learn.

In my life I have never been jealous of the success of others and of the things that other people have. Rather, I was interested in knowing how they could achieve what they wanted. At first I was fascinated by the material things they got, then *I realised that the material goods were prizes that these people gave themselves, rewarding themselves after their efforts.*

But is determination the main cause of the success of many people? Yes, but it is not enough on its own. You can be or seem to be determined in life, but if you want to achieve a goal, or change your lifestyle, it is important to have or to learn the following characteristics of optimistic people which are the basis for every person who wants to achieve success or simply live happily.

Being optimistic is a way of seeing life and this helps you to face your days better. I would like to add that optimism, here, should be understood as a wisdom, learned slowly, from one's own life experiences, as a result of repeated efforts and constant trials. It is useful to compare your past thoughts with your current thoughts, originating from your new actions, understanding that your new thought patterns are now more realistic.

*By learning from your experiences you can remember how you were able to overcome the difficult moments in life, and such memories will help you find the energy and inspiration now and in the future.*

On the other hand, if you have had negative experiences and you have not been able to resolve certain situations, you may start putting difficult questions to yourself which will prove useful in dealing with the past first and then the future while working hard in the present.

I wish to encourage you to find new reasons to make your life happy. You should not judge yourself.

As we know there are past experiences that have often upset us or changed us radically.

*Be compassionate with yourself.*

The next workout is based on several of Seven Covey's books that help people to stay focused on the physical, mental, social/emotional, and spiritual dimensions, keeping balance in their life.

---

**Workout 17**                                    **Date:**

- Are you able to look for good in every situation?

---

- If not what can you do to improve this?

- What did you learn from your past life experiences?

- What solutions did you find?

- Have you tried to talk about your goals with people that you trust? If not, why?

## How to create a positive attitude.

Successful people have learned how to be effective in improving their mindset. You can copy them by following these habits:

1) Believe in your own vision. Be passionate about your project.

2) Practice managing failures and see them as events that you can cope with by using your skills.

3) Learn how to use all of your own resources.

4) Be honest with yourself and listen to your inner voice.

5) Be positive, learning from your experience and failures.

6) Know that the only way is to take initiative and responsibility.

7) Don't return to what hasn't worked on your project or action plan.

8) Don't proceed if your goal isn't linked with your values.

9) Believe you can't please everyone, but you can improve your charisma.

10) Choose a long-term benefit.

11) Get a general idea of things and then proceed, but remember that what you saw, heard and touched doesn't always tell the truth.

12) Be diligent and look deep.

13) Make your inner life determine your external success.

14) Love, love and love without distinction.

**Workout 18**                                **Date:**

**Recognise your attitudes and tick the attitudes that you want to learn.**


Are you able:

- To change?
- To be honest with yourself?
- To do hard work?
- To take risks?
- To manage failures?
- To be passionate?
- To be persistent in your road of achievement?
- To overcome fatigue?
- To manage disappointment?
- To be disciplined?
- To learn new skills?
- To improve your knowledge?
- To increase your courage?
- To Learn from criticism?
- To create good habits?
- To innovate?
- To overcome limits and barriers?
- To be determined?

- To increase your grittiness?

- To stay focused for long hours?

- To manage stress?

- To say no?

- To be humble?

- To ask for help from others?

- To being open minded?

- To overcome adversities?

- To be patient?

- To believe in your strengths?

- To believe in yourself?

**A real example of great attitude and persistence.**

Along the way towards my rebirth one of the models that inspired me is the famous Italian life coach Dr. Cerè, a true icon in the personal development sector, coaching and online business in Italy. I learned how to develop great attitude through the book *Storie Impossibili - Impossible Stories* a book about famous people who have changed their lives with self-control and positive attitude.

A graduate in business administration with substantial experience in the United States, Roberto Cerè is well known for his coaching courses and book publishing activities. Dr. Cerè proudly tells of his rebirth: immersed in debt due to problems related to his past activities, indeed over one hundred and fifty thousand euros, he re-emerged thanks to his tenacity and his knowledge of life and business coaching.

After management consultancy with Arthur Andersen and KPMG, and time as business coach at the

Ferrari Scuderia, Gucci, Mattel and Benetton, Roberto holds highly successful marketing and coaching courses. He is the founder and director of MICAP (International Master in High Performance Coaching), the most complete and demanding study programme in the European market for those who want to become a professional coach. Dr. Cerè has written three bestsellers in Italy and proceeds from the last two were donated to charity. His coaching events have attracted thousands of people. At the last edition of *'Strategie per Coach'* held in Monte Carlo December 2016, over 2000 people were present!

So, how did Dr. Cerè overcome his problems and limits? In the next pages you can read how many people changed their lives!

> **A problem to solve is a resource for discovering your strengths your strengths.**

As you read before, it is possible to learn how to become optimistic and change your beliefs. What can allow you to think and act differently? Your own strengths!

Maybe you have never considered your own strengths as your inner power, the power that can allow you to create a new view of yourself and your life!

Your strengths are the centre of your improvement and change. By using them you will become more and more aware of them and how to use them well, especially when you want to realise your dreams and achieve your goals in life.

*These forces are your personal characteristics that make you unique and are therefore unrepeatable.*

Those who have discovered, managed and developed these strengths have discovered their talents too, fortifying and amplifying themselves through training every day, transforming their acquired skills into talents.

During the dark times of life you can rely on these strengths in such a way as to have inspiration and confirmation of the person you are or want to become. In carefree moments you will be able to enjoy these characteristics of yours as these will be the moments when you express yourself, free even from the concept of time passing just because you will be doing what you like.

I am grateful to Martin Seligman. With his famous twenty-four strengths and values test I discovered who I really am.

Seligman's twenty-four strengths are universal to all human beings and are divided into various areas. According to Seligman, everyone can express and develop these strengths that are personal characteristics. You can consider how to learn and develop them for your human growth, personal and professional development.

You will be surprised to discover your inner potential and you will also be amazed to see these strengths in people around you; indeed, I invite you to discover these characteristics in people without judging them, but whenever possible creating a new opinion of them, also giving you the opportunity to create new relationships.

It is amazing to understand that even if you do not have all of the twenty-four strengths of character, you will have the possibility of integrating and developing those that you hadn't thought of developing. For instance, if you want to develop or improve the characteristic of creativity, at the same time you will also increase the characteristic of curiosity. I have never seen a creative person who is not curious. Have you? And curiosity can lead you to learn more, thus developing the love of knowledge, another characteristic of the virtue of wisdom!

Still, my dear friend, if you have a gap in human relationships and you want to work on yourself, you can start by being kind to other people and even pets; step by step you will discover that you have a different attitude to your neighbours and the people you know. You will develop the desire to give love without receiving anything in return; as you will read, these are characteristics of human virtue.

Our inner strengths are resources in an embryonic state that need to be nurtured, allowing us to improve as individuals. Sometimes it happens that we suffer in life because we do not use our virtues and our strengths of character; it is very important to understand that it is possible to discover their true nature in creating a happy and fulfilled life path.

Another consideration is that many of us are waiting for our retirement to do the things we love, but some of us will never have the joy of following our dreams. We might as well start now. What do you say?

I wish to show you other characteristics of inner strength:

- Your inner power is a potential that, if it is trained, can affect your reality. Through it you can make a subjective and objective change in your life.
- Your competencies are the combination of your personal power and your technical knowledge; know and develop your strengths and know how to train them in achieving your goals and making your life realised.
- Your strengths can develop your talents when a set of your skills can produce excellent results, admirable even by those who are not experts in the field in which it is expressed. And these strengths are the main tools for acquiring new skills.
- You have to experience the mental state of flow; while doing what you like you can forget the passing of time.
**Remember:** your strengths are a trait or traits of your personal character that are combined with your emotions and behaviours which then establish your identity, and identity is connected with your choices, motivations and values.

## Classification and Test on Character Strengths and Virtues.

Based on the studies of Martin Seligman.

Do you know yourself? Do you know your inner power? Do you know your strengths?

To accomplish your goal you need to know what can make the difference in your life and in your project, as C. Peterson and M. Seligman have written in 2004 in their book *Character Strengths and Virtues: A Handbook and Classification,* where they classified the twenty-four strengths of character that are universally recognised in all people in every continent of the world!

You can have all or some of these strengths and you can discover you are stronger or weaker in some of them.

What happens when you don't use your strengths? You can feel sad, demotivated or confused about your goals in life.

If you don't express your strengths completely you can't evaluate your potential in some areas of your life; for instance, if you have hidden your love of knowledge because you have been working hard your entire life, you may suffer unhappiness because you haven't followed your dream and your true interests.

When you know your inner power, you can express yourself in the best way, which can show you who you really are. Discovering your strengths and your values is an opportunity that allows you to live the life that you want.

I wish to invite you to visit the VIA Institute on Character website where it is possible to discover your strengths with the wonderful Free Character Strengths Test and an exhaustive explanation of all the strengths and the main key concepts associated with them.

In addition, you will have the opportunity to train yourself with the Via Institute on Character's exercises and advice.

Let's look at the twenty-four Character Strengths and Virtues, by 'VIA Institute on Character'.

---

## WISDOM.

- Creativity: thinking of new ways to do things is a crucial part of who you are.
- Curiosity: you like exploration and discovery.
- Judgement: you think about things and examine them from all sides.
- Love of Learning: you have a passion for mastering new skills, topics, and bodies of knowledge.
- Perspective: people who know you consider you wise.

## COURAGE.

- Bravery: you don't shrink from threat, challenge, difficulty or pain.
- Honesty: you live your life in a genuine and authentic way.
- Perseverance: you work hard to finish what you start.
- Zest: you approach everything you do with excitement and energy.

---

# HUMANITY.

- Kindness: you are kind and generous to others.
- Love: you value close relations with others.
- Social Intelligence: you know how to fit into different social situations.

# JUSTICE.

- Fairness: one of your abiding principles is to treat all people fairly.
- Leadership: you excel at encouraging a group to get things done.
- Teamwork: you excel as a member of a group.

# TEMPERANCE.

- Forgiveness: you forgive those who have done you wrong.
- Humility: you don't seek the spotlight and others recognise and value your modesty.
- Prudence: you are a careful person.
- Self-regulation: you are a disciplined person.

# TRASCENDENCE.

- Appreciation of Beauty: you notice and appreciate beauty and excellence in all domains of life.
- Gratitude: you are aware of good things that happen and don't take them for granted.
- Hope: you expect the best in the future, and you work to achieve it.
- Humour: bringing smiles to other people is important to you.
- Spirituality: your beliefs shape your actions and are a source of comfort to you.

Take the free Via Institute on Character Test:
http://cristiancairolifecoach.pro.viasurvey.org
Write the link in your browser.
Or visit: www.viacharacter.org

# HOW TO IDENTIFY YOUR WEAKNESSES.

Can your weaknesses limit you? The answer is obvious: your weaknesses can limit you and influence your choices, actions and goals.

Think about how many times you gave up on meeting new partners just because you felt inadequate or shy; think about when you felt insecure about going to a job interview and you missed new opportunities.

Weaknesses can be double-edged weapons; for instance, a dangerous weakness is to overestimate yourself with the consequence of not seeing your behaviour with careful objective analysis.

*Your weaknesses can create a false image of yourself and the reality around you.*

The purpose of this section is to give you the opportunity to assess your weaknesses, firstly accepting them and then taking control when they impact on your life.

136

Understanding who you are is always the first step in your improvement. Examine and compare your beliefs about your weaknesses with what is true in reality. For example, if you think you are shy you will behave as a shy person, but if you gradually realise you have a personality which is just a little closed you can help yourself with appropriate strategies.

Meanwhile, if you are an entrepreneur, clarifying which weaknesses are blocking you on your professional path is the first step to understanding where you have gaps today and reviewing your future plans.

## HOW TO TAKE CONTROL OF YOUR WEAKNESSES.

The next workout gives you a general view of the areas where you are weak, but at the same time it is very useful because you can start to take action in those areas that are blocking your personal development or career.

*It is important not to focus just on the weakness; it is much better to accept them as a big opportunity to go out of your comfort zone, gaining experience little by little and tracking your progress. This will give you another point of view about yourself and your personal power.*

After you have determined the areas that can block you, you can analyse them and work to improve them, transforming them in a positive way. Staying positive is the right way to give yourself the chance to discover the reasons for your weaknesses.

**Workout 19**                                    **Date:**

## MONITORING YOUR PROGRESS.

The weak areas where I can change are:

The main areas where I can make more effort to improve are:

The area that can impact most negatively on my life is:

You can use this model to track your progress. It is a good idea to monitor your progress every month and to repeat the same workout every three months.

Advice to the reader: you may need more sheets of paper for this.

My progress in the First Month:

My progress in the Second Month:

My progress in the Third Month:

My progress in the Sixth Month:

My progress in the Ninth Month:

My progress in the Twelfth Month:

What I discovered about myself during these last months:

# DO YOU KNOW YOUR SKILLS?

I want to explain to you the meaning of the skills that you have or that you want to learn or improve. Which are the skills that you need or want to improve?

**Hard skills.**
When we talk about *hard skills* we are referring to a set of technical skills which can be easily acquired. It all depends on your attitude, on your education, on the specialised courses that you have taken in the past or currently, as well as training experience in the workplace. In fact, hard skills are easily quantifiable and in general they are related to your training experiences or your favourite hobbies.

**Remember:** hard skills can be improved over time and it is possible to transform them into talents.

We can summarise hard skills as:

-the knowledge of one or more foreign languages.

-the use of computer software.

-the use of certain kinds of tools or machinery.

-the specific knowledge that you have in your job area that can interest future employers or companies.

## Academic skills.

This area represents your educational preparation, from your secondary school to degree level and other specialised studies or master's degrees; your academic skills are grouped in with hard skills.

## HARD SKILLS.

Tick the Hard Skills that you have now then identify which ones you would like to have. Add the ones that you have which aren't in this list. Think how you can use them in accordance with your goal.

### Communication Area.

| Listening | Reporting | Persuading |
|-----------|-----------|------------|
| Writing | Drafting | Questioning |
| Training | Editing | Presenting |
| Mediating | Negotiating | Giving Instructions Clearly |

### Customer Service Oriented Area.

| Assisting | Caring | Organising |
|-----------|--------|------------|
| Coaching | Selling | Coordinating |
| Counselling | Servicing Clients | |
| Supporting | Planning | |

146

Thinking and Analysis Area.

| | | |
|---|---|---|
| Analysis | Investigating | Questioning |
| Classifying | Inventing | Researching |
| Evaluating | Learning | Reviewing |
| Problem Solving | Judging | |
| Observing | Suggesting | |

Numerical Skills Area.

| | | |
|---|---|---|
| Accounting | Checking | Measuring |
| Auditing | Accuracy | Recording |
| Budgeting | Compiling | Stocktaking |
| Calculating | Statistics | |
| | Counting | |
| | Estimating | |

Manual Skills Area.

| | | |
|---|---|---|
| Assembling | Inspecting | Protecting |
| Constructing | Loading | Repairing |
| Driving | Operating | Surveying |
| Installing | Producing | |

## Management Skills Area.

| Allocating Duties | Delegating | Motivating |
|---|---|---|
| Appraising | Interviewing | Project Making |
| Coordinating | Leading | Recruiting |
| Decision Making | Managing | |
| | Meetings | |

## My Academic Skills.

**Soft skills.**

*Soft Skills* refer to the interpersonal sphere and your level of communication; these skills are called transversal skills and aren't learned at school or in your workplace.

Soft Skills depend on your personal culture, personality and experience, especially how you interact with your community, family and colleagues.

The usual soft skills are the following:

- flexibility and adaptability in a new context

- problem solving

- motivation and orientation towards achieving goals

- resistance to stress

- time management

- teamwork

- creativity

- attention to details

- being proactive

- assertive skills.

## Interpersonal skills.

These skills are connected to your personality and your life experience, your level of communication and your ability to create relationships with the people around you; interpersonal skills are grouped in with soft skills.

You can practise your hard skills with a specific time schedule and teachers, but it is impossible to do the same with your soft skills because they require certain situations that appear in your life and only you can judge how to learn from them.

Think how you can use, develop or learn more of your current skills in accordance with your goal and your personal development.

| | | |
|---|---|---|
| **Workout 21** | | **Date:** |
| **MY SOFT SKILLS/INTERPERSONAL SKILLS.** | | |

Tick the personal qualities which you have now, then identify which ones you would like to have. Add the ones that you have which aren't in this list. Think how you can use them in accordance with your goal.

| | | |
|---|---|---|
| Accountable | Diligent | Open-Minded |
| Adaptable | Dynamic | Optimistic |
| Analytical | Energetic | Organised |
| Autonomous | Enthusiastic | Practical |
| Challenging | Flexible | Pragmatic |
| Committed | Inclusive | Productive |
| Cooperative | Intuitive | Positive |
| Creative | Logical Thinker | Quality |
| Reliable | | Oriented |
| Resilient | | Versatile |
| Result-Oriented | | |
| Self-Motivated | | |
| Supportive | | |
| Team-Oriented | | |

## DISCOVERING YOUR TALENTS.

*'Your talent comes from your potential,*
*it feeds on it and grows with it.'*

*Cristian Cairo*

Developing your skills, training yourself every day towards perfection, is the beginning of getting great results that will lead you to be a talented person.

This a decisive commitment towards levels of performance that you would never have thought possible before.

I invite you to answer the following questions so you can have valuable thoughts and inspiration.

**Workout 22**                                            **Date:**

*The questions that can change your life for ever.*

What do you do easily and well that is difficult for other people?

153

What is it that you enjoy most about your work?

What kind of big tasks are you able to complete?

What do you really love that you can do well and transform into something truly excellent?

Are you responsible about this, and are you able to understand that deciding to improve your abilities could change your life for ever?

Can you identify what you can do that can make the difference in your work or hobby?

Think how your main strengths can take you forward to excellence.

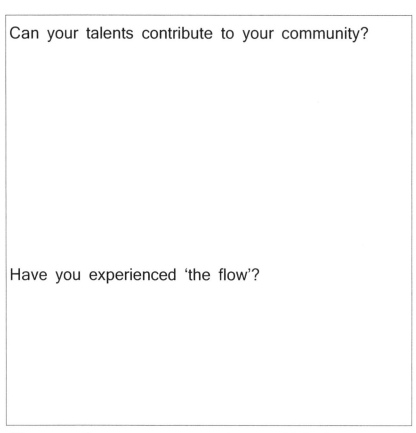

Can your talents contribute to your community?




Have you experienced 'the flow'?




The questions you answered are widely known and used to identify our potentials that can lead us to develop real talents in the areas where we are most capable. *Talent comes from repetitive performance that improves over time with hard training to a perfect fusion of personal strengths, skills, knowledge, assiduous practice, strong motivation and persistence.*

Keep in mind that a talent can also develop under external pressure or impositions with discomfort and suffering. For example, many famous people were pushed and pushed to work very hard when they were young, or we push ourselves because we think that it is the only way we will be respected by others.

A peaceful and profitable environment is ideal to develop your performance. In fact, developing your talent would be almost impossible in a limiting restricting environment, but what allows you to improve is mainly your thoughts, your beliefs and your values. These make the difference when you want to proceed in transforming your skills into talents. The only way to move forward will be to start from a level congenial to you and then gradually increase your performance, monitored with continuous feedback from experts in your sport or profession. In fact, the secret is to do things in the right order, improving step by step every time. It is important to understand that talent needs sacrifices and hard work every day and for ever in a continuous challenge with yourself.

You have to create the right balance between your goal of becoming a talented person and everything else that a good life requires in terms of free time, family and friends. And that's not all, the people around you will have to be ready to understand your intentions and to support you continuously on your long journey towards a life made of sacrifices, but also of enormous satisfactions such as becoming a person who will inspire others' lives and becoming an example of talent!

**Remember:** *talented people are strong enough to deliver their goals through motivation, doing the same things over and over until they achieve their perfection, becoming sure that they have gained the highest level in their field.*

**Workout 23**                                        **Date:**

### Discover your talents!

You can identify your main talents from the following questions so you can have a generic perspective of your talents!

Rate yourself in each area from 1 to 10, where 1 means very weak and 10 is outstanding.

## Task Performance Area.

- Are you an **achiever**? The achiever is a talented person who wants to accomplish a goal in life or in business, working very hard every day. Usually these kind of people are satisfied if they are productive and effective during their tasks.

| 1 | 2 | 3 | 4 | 5 | 6 | 7 | 8 | 9 | 10 |
|---|---|---|---|---|---|---|---|---|----|

- Do you like being organised or organising something? If you like to arrange something this is because you have a talent in organising tasks or things in a detailed way. Are you an **organiser**?

| 1 | 2 | 3 | 4 | 5 | 6 | 7 | 8 | 9 | 10 |
|---|---|---|---|---|---|---|---|---|----|

- When you trust people around you or you believe it is possible to do anything in life, it is because you feel like a **believer,** a person who has deep resources to achieve goals or lead people. Do you agree with this description?

| 1 | 2 | 3 | 4 | 5 | 6 | 7 | 8 | 9 | 10 |
|---|---|---|---|---|---|---|---|---|----|

- What is the best quality of someone like you? When you give your word you mean it, and you treat people with fairness? Surely you belong to the category of **consistent** people, don't you?

| 1 | 2 | 3 | 4 | 5 | 6 | 7 | 8 | 9 | 10 |
|---|---|---|---|---|---|---|---|---|----|

- Or do you belong to the category of people who like order and at the same time follow **discipline** as a lifestyle and also at work?

| 1 | 2 | 3 | 4 | 5 | 6 | 7 | 8 | 9 | 10 |
|---|---|---|---|---|---|---|---|---|----|

- Are you appreciated by people around you for your ability to decide or make choices? It is probable that they like your excellent **decision-making** skills.

| 1 | 2 | 3 | 4 | 5 | 6 | 7 | 8 | 9 | 10 |
|---|---|---|---|---|---|---|---|---|----|

-And that's not all, surely they trust you because you are a reliable and **responsible** person. In fact, do you have a position of responsibility?

| 1 | 2 | 3 | 4 | 5 | 6 | 7 | 8 | 9 | 10 |
|---|---|---|---|---|---|---|---|---|----|

- At this point, I would say that you are an exceptional person with so many qualities that if I were a manager I would hire you right away! One of the most sought after skills today in the world of work is the ability to stay **focused** for a long time in situations of high stress where you need to make decisions, and above all have the ability to continue to stay focused on long-term goals. Are you able stay focused in different contexts under pressure?

| 1 | 2 | 3 | 4 | 5 | 6 | 7 | 8 | 9 | 10 |
|---|---|---|---|---|---|---|---|---|----|

- Sometimes it isn't easy to find solutions, however you can always train yourself. A person talented in **problem solving** is always required, as well as being helpful in your daily life. Do you think you have this talent?

| 1 | 2 | 3 | 4 | 5 | 6 | 7 | 8 | 9 | 10 |
|---|---|---|---|---|---|---|---|---|----|

# Influencer Area

Today it is very easy to know somebody that is famous because they are called an 'influencer'; in general, an influencer is a professional who is able to persuade other people to buy a product or service, or to invite them to follow certain ideas or campaigns.

In certain ways you can be an influencer in your job and in your own environment. The following questions will help you to evaluate if you have talents in this area.

- Uhm... if you are impatient to make something happen and you are able to transform your ideas into actions with a clear vision, I think you are an **activator** like me! Do you recognise yourself in this description?

| 1 | 2 | 3 | 4 | 5 | 6 | 7 | 8 | 9 | 10 |
|---|---|---|---|---|---|---|---|---|----|
|   |   |   |   |   |   |   |   |   |    |

- Do you know that sometimes you need to take control of the situation around you, such as at work or in your family? If this event doesn't scare you can you take decisions with responsibility? If your answer is positive you have the talent of **command.**

| 1 | 2 | 3 | 4 | 5 | 6 | 7 | 8 | 9 | 10 |
|---|---|---|---|---|---|---|---|---|----|
|   |   |   |   |   |   |   |   |   |    |

- When was the last time you were amazed by a good leader with the power of both command and communication? To be an effective **communicator** is one the most important skills requested by H.R. offices.

| 1 | 2 | 3 | 4 | 5 | 6 | 7 | 8 | 9 | 10 |
|---|---|---|---|---|---|---|---|---|----|

To be a good **speaker** is the talent to put your thoughts into words clearly, and this power will be appreciated in every area of your life. Think how many problems you can solve with this talent, when you discuss something with your partner for instance! Are you able to speak in public in a natural way?

| 1 | 2 | 3 | 4 | 5 | 6 | 7 | 8 | 9 | 10 |
|---|---|---|---|---|---|---|---|---|----|

- Have you had arguments with your partner or friend because you always want to win in any competition? Do you like to compete against others? Maybe you have a natural talent in the **competition area**.

| 1 | 2 | 3 | 4 | 5 | 6 | 7 | 8 | 9 | 10 |
|---|---|---|---|---|---|---|---|---|----|

- In general, someone who has these skills could have developed the talent of **maximiser**, because it is possible for them to transform their own or others' strengths into something truly excellent. Do you like to transform others' lives positively through their own inner powers?

| 1 | 2 | 3 | 4 | 5 | 6 | 7 | 8 | 9 | 10 |
|---|---|---|---|---|---|---|---|---|---|

- Do you feel confident enough to manage your life, making decisions and following them with strong determination under all circumstances? It is possible that you have the talent of **self-assurance**!

| 1 | 2 | 3 | 4 | 5 | 6 | 7 | 8 | 9 | 10 |
|---|---|---|---|---|---|---|---|---|---|

- In our lives it is important to find a vision that can drive us to live with **meaning**, and this is one of the pillars in making your life happy and realised despite the difficulties that you may meet every day. Do you have aims in your life and do you want to create a life with meaning?

| 1 | 2 | 3 | 4 | 5 | 6 | 7 | 8 | 9 | 10 |
|---|---|---|---|---|---|---|---|---|---|

- Can you identify a person who has influenced your life with **charisma**? Do you like to meet new people and create good connections with them? If the answer is affirmative, well, you are appreciated for your charismatic and human qualities. Congratulations!

| 1 | 2 | 3 | 4 | 5 | 6 | 7 | 8 | 9 | 10 |
|---|---|---|---|---|---|---|---|---|---|

## Relationships Area

With your charisma you can easily work with others and form rewarding relationships, and your presence is appreciated especially by those who want to achieve goals alongside you. Do you think you are good **relator**?

| 1 | 2 | 3 | 4 | 5 | 6 | 7 | 8 | 9 | 10 |
|---|---|---|---|---|---|---|---|---|---|

- According to numerous academic researchers having a positive character can impact positively in every area of your life and it can help you to create good connections with others; in fact, someone who has the ability to create strong relationships keeping their team together is able to make the team bigger than the sum of its parts, enhancing each person in the team. Do you have the talent of being **positive** despite external events?

| 1 | 2 | 3 | 4 | 5 | 6 | 7 | 8 | 9 | 10 |
|---|---|---|---|---|---|---|---|---|---|

- Being an excellent and positive leader requires you to be conscious that each person around you has inner powers that need to be discovered. Do you think you have this quality, and are you able to support others with your talent of **individualisation**?

| 1 | 2 | 3 | 4 | 5 | 6 | 7 | 8 | 9 | 10 |
|---|---|---|---|---|---|---|---|---|----|

- Is your goal to keep people together, like family and friends or colleagues? Do you like to create **harmony** and avoid conflicts? To have this talent is very helpful nowadays, especially when your team faces challenges or when your family has to overcome a difficult situation.

| 1 | 2 | 3 | 4 | 5 | 6 | 7 | 8 | 9 | 10 |
|---|---|---|---|---|---|---|---|---|----|

- When is a team strong or when is your family united? When every person feels included. Are you able to allow every person in your group to express themselves, including those who risk being left out in your proposal or challenge? Maybe you are a talented **includer**.

| 1 | 2 | 3 | 4 | 5 | 6 | 7 | 8 | 9 | 10 |
|---|---|---|---|---|---|---|---|---|----|

- Being an includer is easy because you have developed another much appreciated talent: **empathy** for others. Can you make a difference around you using this talent?

| 1 | 2 | 3 | 4 | 5 | 6 | 7 | 8 | 9 | 10 |
|---|---|---|---|---|---|---|---|---|----|

- As you have read in the Relationships Area, many talents work together. In fact, it is almost impossible not to have one or more talents in this area, and you could develop all these talents during your lifetime.

For instance, for me it is important that the people around me are happy and are able to feel realised, creating the life they want. In fact, I decided to become a Life Coach because I wanted to support others in accomplishing their goals. My talent as a **developer** has helped me to recognise others' inner strengths giving them the satisfaction of enjoying their achieved vision. Do you have a similar talent?

| 1 | 2 | 3 | 4 | 5 | 6 | 7 | 8 | 9 | 10 |
|---|---|---|---|---|---|---|---|---|----|

- My proposal is possible only if I am able to create a **connection** with the people around me and the environment where I live, having an open mind that allows me to find a connection with the world.

Could you say the same thing about yourself? Are you able to create connections with the people around you and all creatures in nature?

| 1 | 2 | 3 | 4 | 5 | 6 | 7 | 8 | 9 | 10 |
|---|---|---|---|---|---|---|---|---|----|

- Creating good relationships and making connections with the world around you is possible if you have the awareness to adapt to circumstances with flexibility and have the courage to know how to wait for the right time when things are in your favour; taking care to seize opportunities in life and work is a talent that will open up many doors in the future. Think deeply about this gift of yours and thank yourself for having developed it. Are you **adaptable** in different circumstances?

| 1 | 2 | 3 | 4 | 5 | 6 | 7 | 8 | 9 | 10 |
|---|---|---|---|---|---|---|---|---|----|

# Strategic Thinking

- If you are among those people who love to learn and read a lot with the intention of storing information for future use, you are welcome! Nowadays knowing how to choose the right information is almost an art, given the amount of news, blogs and video tutorials that circulate around us every day. Can you evaluate the acquired information you need, deciding what is useful for you to know? If you can do this, you have a talent in the **input area.**

| 1 | 2 | 3 | 4 | 5 | 6 | 7 | 8 | 9 | 10 |
|---|---|---|---|---|---|---|---|---|----|
|   |   |   |   |   |   |   |   |   |    |

- A talent that I envy is the **analytical capacity**; being good at understanding the origin and cause of things and events is useful in every area of life. In addition, it is a useful skill for those who use foresight in their choice of life and work. Are you able to foresee events and situations? Well, you are a resource for your community.

| 1 | 2 | 3 | 4 | 5 | 6 | 7 | 8 | 9 | 10 |
|---|---|---|---|---|---|---|---|---|----|
|   |   |   |   |   |   |   |   |   |    |

- Maybe you have developed your analytical capacity because you have trained your critical thinking, reaching a clear vision of the present time, drawing on important details from past history. Usually people with this talent are able to **evaluate** different **contexts**. Do you think you have this talent?

| 1 | 2 | 3 | 4 | 5 | 6 | 7 | 8 | 9 | 10 |
|---|---|---|---|---|---|---|---|---|----|

- Knowing the past and the present can inspire you to find new solutions in the future which no one has thought of before. Usually people with this talent are charismatic and they inspire confidence given their vision of an alternative future. They always desire to propose new things. Do you inspire and energise people close to you with ideas that are **futuristic** and alternative?

| 1 | 2 | 3 | 4 | 5 | 6 | 7 | 8 | 9 | 10 |
|---|---|---|---|---|---|---|---|---|----|

- Having **futuristic talent** is ideal for people who are able to make things happens, because they can visualise new ideas and solutions realising them with energy. They can find new connections between different things or situations. Do you often get lots of ideas and make them happen?

You have a talent in the area of **ideation.**

| 1 | 2 | 3 | 4 | 5 | 6 | 7 | 8 | 9 | 10 |
|---|---|---|---|---|---|---|---|---|----|

- Often people with lots of ideas are lucky enough to have the love of knowledge and are at ease even on their own as long as they are in the presence of something to learn, but if the opportunity presents itself to learn new things with other people they are very happy. Do you have this feature? The **learning talent** is common to all successful people and it is the best way to improve yourself.

| 1 | 2 | 3 | 4 | 5 | 6 | 7 | 8 | 9 | 10 |
|---|---|---|---|---|---|---|---|---|----|

- A talent that I will never give up is **strategic talent.** In fact, I can always find alternatives and new ways to deal with problems, finding new solutions even in difficult contexts. Do you like to find new solutions and experiment with new paths?

| 1 | 2 | 3 | 4 | 5 | 6 | 7 | 8 | 9 | 10 |
|---|---|---|---|---|---|---|---|---|----|

- Once upon a time introspective people were seen as eccentric, but nowadays even an assertive leader can have the **talent of intellect** and is able to support intellectual discussion with countless advantages for his team. Do you think the same about yourself?

| 1 | 2 | 3 | 4 | 5 | 6 | 7 | 8 | 9 | 10 |
|---|---|---|---|---|---|---|---|---|----|

**Workout 24**                                          **Date:**

Write down your talents and think how to use them or improve them:

## CONSIDERATIONS ABOUT YOUR FIRST STEP:

In this first step you had the opportunity to discover yourself through your strengths and weaknesses and the limitations that can block your personal development and your projects.

With your strengths you can develop your talents which can transform you, making the difference in others' lives.

It is important to understand which beliefs can keep you far away from your personal vision; the best strategy is to evaluate your current thinking patterns, transforming them into positive thinking patterns.

Taking control of your thoughts and actions can allow you to achieve more in life, becoming the master of your destiny.

Every six months you can re-read the chapter about the first step, because it is very useful, especially when you feel you are losing your energy or motivation. Reading this step many times will allow you to discover more and more about yourself!

## THE SECOND STEP.

### WHAT DO YOU WANT?

'People with goals succeed because they know where they're going.'

                                Florence Nightingale

What do you want? What do you want to become? These are two questions that we ask ourselves frequently in life, even as children.

Sometimes we are ready to respond because we already know the answer, even though we ask ourselves these questions. It often happens that you aren't able to respond, or you are undecided about the answer. As they are very personal questions, we can experience them with anguish, frustration, confusion and doubt, which doesn't help us in feeling calm and focused. How can we find the answers we need?

The next workout shows four quadrants in which are represented the four typical situations that we encounter when we have to respond to ourselves or to other people about what we want to accomplish in life... and sometimes about what kind of pizza we would like!

## YOU...

| Know what you want. | Don't you know what you want. |
|---|---|
| Have given up on your dreams. | Are delegating or waiting for something to happen in your life. |

**You know what you want.**

Knowing what you want is the first step towards the realisation of your goal. You will certainly encounter obstacles along the way, but by going through the following chapters you will be able to overcome them by doing an action plan related to your ideas.

**You don't know what you want.**

Not knowing what you want is a situation that arises very often in life. The important thing is not to try to find a solution immediately or at any cost. So what can you do instead?

Maybe you have many opportunities to choose from and, not knowing which is right for you, you might remain undecided and confused.

Instead, if you are really sure that you don't know what you want, try asking yourself: how well do you really know yourself?

Do you really know your skills and your dreams?

The workouts that I propose are a precious way of clarifying what we want and who we are, step by step.

A valid help is to understand if you have renounced some of your dreams or part of the desire to be fulfilled, or if you have partly forgotten who you are and what you want from life. Ask for help from experienced people such as Life Coaches or Counsellors who are prepared to support you in your personal search.

Maybe you have received a series of negative feedbacks that have influenced you, limiting your choices.

Try again to clarify your own needs, desires and dreams while listening to your heart.

**You are delegating or waiting for something to happen in your life.**

Are you delegating your happiness to events or people around you? Are you waiting for something to happen in your life?

Can you be patient even when you are on the path to happiness and self-realisation while waiting for events to favour you?

I want to give you an example based on my own life: I waited many years to find something that could give me a reason to live the life I wanted; I was so confused, unhappy and angry with myself. What could I do?

I learned not to just follow my dreams; in fact, I gave importance to the benefits from my experience, good or bad! I learned that it was important to respect myself and accept the things about me that I didn't want to see as my dark side.

I risked delegating my life to my false beliefs and to the image that I created to satisfy others' expectations or judgement. People told me that I was too small and weak to have a life like other teenagers. At school I was bullied by a group of classmates and later on even in certain workplaces. Step by step I accepted myself, viewing what was beautiful in me as a person, and I decided that it was much better to resist my sadness and not to fight against the bullies. I discovered myself with meditation and by helping others, especially supporting old people, learning from their wisdom how it is possible to live better and have good relations with other people.

If you delegate your choices and your life to other people and events, be aware of your thoughts and personal beliefs; start to think that it's time to analyse the reasons for your choices, or the motivations for delegating your life to others' decisions or their judgements.

We often delegate our choices in a non-conscious way. In fact, we make decisions that are apparently conscious and well-defined and which we believe to be correct, but in reality we hide from other solutions that we don't want to see at the moment.

For example, if we plan to go abroad is it because we want to have new and exciting experiences or because are we fleeing from something that makes us suffer? Or are we blocking ourselves from responsibilities that we don't want to take? Our subconscious can drive our decisions and actions creating false answers to 'protect us' from suffering.

**You have given up on your dreams.**

What does the phrase 'giving up your goals' mean to you?

According to your answer to this question, you can understand what you need to change or improve, and the reasons why you have given up on your goals.

It is possible to consider your past mistakes as a form of teaching, showing you where you went wrong and understanding different possible solutions that you could have applied before.

Don't judge yourself or see yourself through others' judgement, but try to evaluate yourself and the situations that happened to you as an opportunity to transform your life.

Try to understand where you could improve or change your life and where it is possible to avoid certain kinds of people or situations until you find the energy and strength to deal with them.

Sometimes we give up for a number of reasons. For instance, when you decide to live far away from your relatives and friends you might give up because you could be worried about living alone or because you would miss them.

Maybe giving up on your plan could hide a lack of self-confidence, or it may be influenced by other circumstances that occur suddenly and which produce a profound and radical change in you.

*The nature of your giving up has influenced your choices and your goals afterwards. You need to understand it is important not to repeat the same condition and situation in the future.*

*And this is the greatest fear: not being able to obtain anything from our lives because we do not deserve it or being so sure that we will never find other motivations or other energies to be used in realising our desires and objectives.*

This book can give you examples, suggestions and valid workouts to help you understand what motivations have led you to give up on your goals, and at the same time to lead you on a new and exciting pathway where you can start to renew yourself and your life!

As Laura Nash and Howard Stevenson wrote in their famous book *Just Enough: Tools for Creating Success in Your Work and Life,* you need to pay attention to more than one area of your life (exactly as you have seen in the three main areas - Competence, Relationships and Autonomy), deciding what is really important to you. Their work shows that your success has to be sustainable across the four main areas of self, family, success and your community, and within them you have to consider the following important components: *happiness, achievement, meaning and legacy.* These components relate to each other but they can impact on your life in different ways and you can decide how to manage and improve them.

The four components.

| Happiness | Achievement | Meaning | Legacy |
|-----------|-------------|---------|--------|

+

The four areas of life.

| Self | Family | Work | Community |
|------|--------|------|-----------|

It is important to understand clearly the connection between the goals in the four components and the four areas in your life. Use the boxes above to evaluate if you can improve your current situation by considering all the components and areas together, or by deciding to spend more energy on one of them at a time, creating equilibrium between the areas that you need to change or develop.

# THE WHEEL OF LIFE.

Another useful workout to evaluate and reflect on your current situation and understand how to direct your future is the Wheel of Life.

The Wheel of Life is a tool used in Life Coaching and Management Coaching to define life or job priorities. In the Wheel of Life the areas of life are shown in greater detail. In fact, as you can see the areas are divided into many themes: personal development, business and career, money and finance, contribution to the community, relationships, romance, health, fun and spare time.

*Basically, your analysis will be even more detailed, giving you the opportunity to act more precisely in the areas of your life that interest you the most.*

The Wheel of Life has the same principles as the Competence, Relationships & Autonomy workout; you will give a rating from 1 to 10.

Keep in mind that your rating is influenced by your current situation, by what you think about yourself and what others see in you. *The Wheel of Life is a good indicator that shows how you see yourself in the future.*

With the Wheel of Life it is possible to understand where you are going in your life. In fact, you can use it for your past time, your present time and your future time.

You can evaluate your present time where it is possible to define your current situation and to establish which areas are weak or which ones you don't pay attention to.

Just thinking of your present time isn't enough because you need to consider your past too. Analyse your past from about five or ten years ago. This can give you a view of your current situation, your behaviours, habits and the beliefs that you still hold.

Making an evaluation of your past can allow you to remember how you have overcome difficulties or how you have given up trying to solve certain problems and how it can influence your present and your future if you don't decide to change your beliefs and take appropriate action in time.

*The Wheel of Life is an excellent tool that allows you to rethink and reproject your future, viewing the precise direction you want to go and discovering new vision and new goals in your life.*

**Always remember:** don't judge yourself severely and above all be ready for change; complete the Wheel of Life workout because it gives you the opportunity to see your current situation and write a realistic action plan to attain the new life for which you feel a burning desire.

I suggest you find a quiet place without disturbances and concentrate during the workout. Write the results in your logbook with the date of this exercise so you have a timeline for your progress.

Example:

## My Wheel of Life.

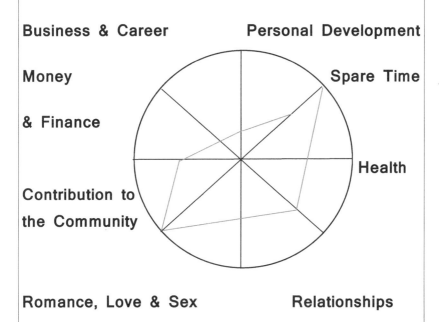

Business & Career          Personal Development

Money                              Spare Time

& Finance

                                        Health

Contribution to
the Community

Romance, Love & Sex          Relationships

In this example I rated each area and have drawn lines to complete the diagram. In this case my leisure time is well developed and I am happy with it. But I spend too long in the pub, ballrooms and restaurants, drinking a lot of alcohol and food and rarely exercise. So my fitness and health are weak as are my money and finances. Fortunately, it is a fantasy example and it isn't related to me!

In the other areas you can see that romance, love and sex are fine, but unfortunately it is always a fantasy example…

**Workout 25**                            **Date:**

## A Picture of Your Life with the Wheel of Life.

### (Your Wheel of Life.)

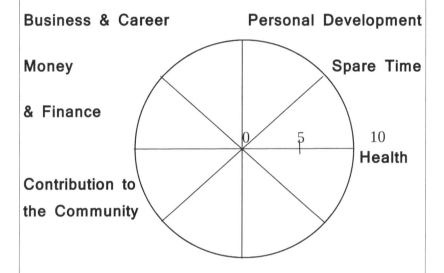

**Business & Career**          **Personal Development**

**Money**

**& Finance**

0      5      10

**Spare Time**

**Health**

**Contribution to**

**the Community**

**Romance, Love & Sex**          **Relationships**

Keep a record of your personal development with three different Wheels of Life related to your past, your current situation and your future. Then repeat the same workout every six months. You will need to copy this workout to past, present and future then record your workouts in your logbook.

# CREATE YOUR NEW LIFE WITH THE C.A.I.R.O. METHOD ©

The C.A.I.R.O. Method is an excellent way to understand what we can do to change our lives, taking into account that we do not always need to make big changes. In reality not everything we want requires the same approach. Sometimes it is enough to add new things, new activities, new mental schemes or new relationships to have a full and happy life. Our task is to assess accurately what we already have or what we have achieved in the various areas of life, and to understand what we can add later. If changing a situation - a job or a relationship requires a lot of effort - we can consider improving the situation that we already have. For example, if we want to make a career it may not always be necessary to find a new job. Instead we could evaluate whether in our current work there is the possibility of improving, perhaps with courses or training. In this way we will have acquired new skills, advancing in our career without changing our current job. Let us always ask ourselves how we can improve certain situations rather than abandoning them or changing them drastically for something different. On the other hand we can remove anything that hinders us or makes us unhappy or unmotivated. We can ask ourselves if it is worthwhile to keep on doing the same things all the time which do not bring us benefits or results; often, and through bad habits, we risk nullifying our dreams and efforts. So it will be better to remove what limits us. Once we have understood where and how to intervene we can create new options. Learning to evaluate the opportunities we encounter and to create new paths allows us to make the life we want and deserve. We can also use the C.A.I.R.O. Method to improve our goals, using it both in goals setting and in our action plan as it will be essential to make changes, additions, improvements and cancellations to our goals along the way - always finding new options.

# CREATE YOUR LIFE

## WITH THE C.A.I.R.O. METHOD ©

**Workout 26**                                    **Date:**

- **CHANGE:** take the power to control your life in those areas that you want to change completely or in part.

- **ADD**: doing new activities and planning new goals to create a fulfilling and challenging life.

- **IMPROVE**: what you already have, learning how to appreciate it.

- **REMOVE:** removing activities, situations or people that block your happiness or delay your self-improvement.

- **OPTIONS:** find new options that can give you a new view about your life and goals.

# THE CHARACTERISTICS OF A GOOD GOAL.

| | |
|---|---|
| PERSONAL | SPECIFIC |
| CHALLENGING | MEASURABLE |
| CLEAR | ATTAINABLE |
| DETAILED | REALISTIC |
| ORGANISED into SUB-GOALS | TIMELY with a timeframe. |

A good goal has the characteristic shown in the table above, and it can help you to understand better what you want and how to create your goal step by step.

I would also add that the table list is useful both for those who have a clear goal and for those who don't know what to target but are looking for something that in some way may sooner or later inspire them.

Let's proceed in order and see what a good goal should be like.

## YOUR GOAL HAS TO BE PERSONAL.

Do you remember that I had mentioned the importance of the fact that a goal must be chosen and decided by you? Well, that's right!
Your goal must be personal, that is, chosen and ardently desired by you. Don't simply follow others but be inspired by positive models.

## YOUR GOAL HAS TO BE CHALLENGING.

What is a goal if it does not give us the energy or the appetite to reach it? Therefore, your goal must above all be challenging.
If there is no 'appetite' for the challenge, sooner or later you will get tired of your goal, with the risk of finding yourself demotivated and without interest in it and with probable low self-esteem for not being able to achieve what you had set out to do. Do not worry, it is always possible to back up and look for other challenging goals.

## YOUR GOAL HAS TO BE CLEAR.

Another feature is that the clearer your goal is the more effective it will be in the next steps. For example, if you say, 'I want to be a millionaire,' it's not a clear goal. It is just a dream.

Let's see how to proceed. First of all formulate the goal you want to reach in the present tense and use positive words which simply describe what you want, being more specific: 'I am a happy millionaire who has one million dollars in the bank.'

By changing the perspective your mind begins to feel the benefits of the feeling of physically having that money in the bank. Moreover, having formulated and visualised one million dollars makes you feel satisfied and excited.

But that's not enough to make your goal clear, is it? Try to say with a big smile on your lips and expressing happiness with your gestures:

'Well, yes! I am a happy millionaire with one million dollars earned with my big idea of selling my product on the Internet!'

How did you feel while saying this sentence? Feelings and emotions are important because they suggest that your goal is clear for you; force yourself to write down your clear goal right away!

## YOUR GOAL HAS TO BE DETAILED.

It's fun to describe your goal, isn't it? It's time to put in the details that your project needs. You could use your goal now instead of following my example (with the millionaire).

Once you have your goal clearly in mind you must write down all the details. If you don't know how to proceed have a look at similar projects and ask people with experience in that area. Keep in mind that the more details you put in the easier it will be to realise your goal. It is like doing a shopping list so you don't forget to buy something!

*In this phase it is better to proceed from the end of your goal:*

*in practice you have to start from the end and proceed backwards, describing all the necessary steps without neglecting anything, until you get to the first step.*

You'll always have time to double check it all at a later date, and you'll be able to modify your plan at any time or put in new things never thought of before.

- Start from the end and proceed backwards.
- Write down all details about your goal.
- Have a look at similar goals or ask experts.
- Double check your goal and modify it at any time.
- Keep a notebook where you can write down new ideas to add to your goal!

## YOUR GOAL HAS TO BE ORGANISED INTO SUB-GOALS!

Are you worried about an overly large or complex goal, or maybe you don't know how to organise all the details of your project?

By dividing your goal into several parts you will have more control over it and you will have a clear distinct guide on the steps to take with the advantage of not being 'too scared' by a goal that is too big or too long in duration.

# WHAT DOES S.M.A.R.T. MEAN?

## S.M.A.R.T. MEANS...

**S**pecific, significant, stretching.

**M**easurable, meaningful, motivational.

**A**greed upon, achievable, action-oriented.

**R**elevant, result-oriented, rewarding.

**T**imeframe, time-bound, trackable.

We can use another popular method to have a clearer idea about our goal. With S.M.A.R.T. you will have a map of those characteristics that a good goal must have. These characteristics have been widely known and used since antiquity to design or create goals.

## YOUR GOAL HAS TO BE SPECIFIC.

Your goal must be specific. This feature helps you to focus on both the ideas and the resources you will use when acting. Having a confused goal is not useful; rather, clarify what you want the most and try to think more efficiently. Take care to be focused when you think about your goal. With a specific goal you have more chance of achieving it than with a general and undefined goal; it is like going somewhere and knowing your destiny clearly.

## YOUR GOAL HAS TO BE MEASURABLE.

Having a specific goal you benefit as you have a sure route to follow, and not only that, in fact, you can **measure** the performances that will allow you to realise your project. For example, it is very useful to know how many kilograms you must lose or gain on your diet; with measurable data you will have parameters on which you can commit yourself, instead of thinking about losing or gaining pounds without knowing their exact quantity.

Having a clear idea where to start and where to get to will help you be even more organised.

## YOUR GOAL HAS TO BE ATTAINABLE.

Using the example from before, and knowing with certainty how many kilograms you will lose or gain during your diet, the possibility to evaluate this type of objective is reachable. For example, if you think about losing two kilograms in a day it is almost impossible and physically harmful; if you think about losing ten kilograms in a month without changing your eating habits, I see it as an impossible goal and therefore an unreachable challenge. Having an attainable goal and following our abilities is the first step to follow.

The steps that you will take are steps created by you through your attitudes, abilities, skills, time and technical equipment that allow you to see your goal as **Attainable**. This will be possible because you have understood that you can reach your goal with the right mindset, such as learning new things, improving yourself and developing your strengths.

Now you can transform your idea in something **Realistic**!

## YOUR GOAL HAS TO BE REALISTIC.

Another feature that I have always found useful is to create achievable and realistic goals. It often happens that we confuse the two terms. In fact, it is possible to realise everything we want, but unfortunately not everything is feasible. An example is the discovery of new planets in our solar system; on the one hand, at a theoretical level, humanity will be able to discover and populate new planets in the future, since we will have the scientific resources for this step, but then, as often happens in reality, external events or circumstances will clash with the idea removing this dream. This was an extreme example to help give you the right target for your projects, the difference between desires, dreams and projects lies precisely in seeing the concrete possibility of being able to realise what was thought of.

# YOUR GOAL HAS TO HAVE A TIMEFRAME.

The last but not the least characteristic is connected to the temporality and duration of your goal. Remember, every project, even the most accurate one or the most grandiose objective without an adequate duration or execution date, remains a dream.

You may well have in mind every detail of your goal and know that it is achievable, but not setting a date within which to complete it will not give you the opportunity to see it realised, as you will not know when to start and when to finish your project.

**Remember:** a goal needs to be reached within a period of time that can vary with the difficulty of realising it. Without a clear **Timeframe** it is very hard to make your goal happen.

This book is written following the S.M.A.R.T. principle, and now you have a map that can drive you on your road to success, a road to success that has different steps where it is possible to measure your progress and your improvement with several criteria to reach your sub-goals and your final goal, following the right steps with the actions and the efforts required to reach your goal.

**Minimal Goal, Transitional Goals and Maximum Goal.**

When you want to set up your goal it has to follow the S.M.A.R.T. characteristics according to what you want to achieve; without these conditions your goal will be a mere dream in the drawer.

Maybe you are asking yourself the next question: can I apply such premises to all kinds of goals? Yes, but we must make a distinction.
You can apply these characteristics to all types of your goals but you need to pay attention to their **nature**.

I'll give you an example: if your goal is to study ten pages every day for your geography exam at the end of the month, it will be different from making a longer study plan such as choosing your future subject at university. In that case you will have to choose your subject carefully from the thousands currently available and know how to choose the best university for you. But that's not all. You could find your university in another city or in a different country from yours.

Finding yourself facing new people, things and situations all at once, your emotions, your energy and your experiences will be completely different from simply studying for a geography exam.

As you have understood from the examples, these two goals have a different nature and your first task is to understand the nature of your goal and behave accordingly; in fact, you will make different efforts for different goals.

You will be faced with a **Minimal Goal** when achieving it does not require much energy or concentration over the long term. Usually with a *Minimal Goal* your performance will be sufficient to reach your goal and you won't have to burden yourself with excessive tasks and efforts as in the example you read about 'ten pages a day to study for your geography exam', which is an easy goal and does not require great effort, at least in a short-term period.

While achieving your desired degree you will have to face a series of difficulties never met before, but luckily not all together at the same time. In fact, it will be necessary to create intermediate or *Transitional Goals*. For instance, if you are still studying at secondary school you could plan to do other courses or study a new language useful for your future university studies, and before that you will have to successfully complete your studies at school!

In the case of a young salesman who aspires to become an area manager, he will have to plan a series of minimum goals and a series of transitional goals before his final goal. He will have to learn how to sell, how to overcome the objections of his clients, he has to know the products very well, and to plan his work trips by car, etc. Later he will learn how to manage a small group of sales people and how to support and motivate them every day. As you are coming to understand, he is faced with different goals which require different time periods, efforts and capacities that will lead the young salesman towards his Maximum Goal. Becoming an area leader in this case is an example of a **Maximum Goal.**

**Remember:** in life you can plan a lot of minimum goals and transitional goals but only a few maximum goals... but who knows? You can say: 'everything will depend on me.'
So, which is your first important goal?

# WHICH IS YOUR FIRST IMPORTANT GOAL?

If you have more than one goal, choose the main goals that you want to achieve from now and decide which is the most important goal, which represents your burning desire!

Make a list and choose only three goals that you consider really important then start from the most important one to you.

Keep this workout in your logbook and you will have a view of your desires, dream, vision and goals at any time.
It is like your best friend, and when you feel confused or unhappy or demotivated you can look at your goal list and define your vision and motivation better.
A good idea is to write your goal down on many Post-it notes and spread them around you.

**Workout 27**                                    **Date:**

My GOALS are:



My three important goals that I want to realise from
now are:
1)


2)


3)


Of these my most important goal is:

## VISUALISE YOUR GOAL.

Now it is time to give your mind the power to reach your desires.

Use your imagination to help you to attain your goals, paying attention to your intuition which will always lead you towards your dream. In fact our dreams and actions are connected; imagining your goal being achieved is the first step.

You have to learn how to increase your imagination, because you have to distinguish a mere dream from an imagined idea that will become real in your life; it is important not to have just a vague abstract idea, but you have to learn how to visualise it to make it concrete.

Prepare your mind for action. It is not as difficult as it may seem.

I would suggest you visualise your goal and if you have more than one, it is prudent to pay attention to one goal at a time, maybe starting from the most important!

Here there is the sequence that helps you to visualise your goal and all its features that you will use later in the following workout, where you will write what you want to achieve in your life.

- find a quiet place where you can be alone and without any disturbance.

- turn off any source of annoyance, such as mobile phones, television or radio, and if you have the washing machine in action... wait for it to stop.

- lean back on your chair and relax.

- relax and allow your muscles to feel no pain or fatigue during the exercise.

- when you have found your position, close your eyes and begin to imagine your goal is real and has just been achieved. You are happy because you feel energised having given your best in allowing yourself to achieve your goal!

- try to let yourself go to your emotions and feelings and discover how good it is to live with what you have just achieved. Savour the moment with your family, friends and with those who have helped you in this new challenge.
- the more concentrated you are the more details you can use. Details that will help you to write your goal better. So, try to capture:
- details about your project
- the tasks that need to be done
- places
- and people.

When you have imagined 'the journey backwards' with all useful elements and the sensations of your experience, you will have an idea about how to plan your goal, how to cope with it and how to manage any problems that you will meet in the future.

The emotions and feelings that you experienced can make you ready to manage the dark moments during your project.

| Write what you want to achieve in your life. |
| --- |

Once you have finished viewing your goal, you must immediately write down what you have 'done' during your visualisation.

Write down a summary about your goal in your **logbook** so as to have a tangible point of reference; in fact, it's a bit like if your goal started to come to life, little by little in reality. Think of the projects and drawings of the architects or engineers who, step by step, plan what they imagined making it visible to all of us in reality.

It is the same for you when you write down your goal and it appears in your reality because is written on a white sheet.

In addition, you can know at every moment of your day what to do and how to do it.

*In this first phase it is not necessary to write down all you need for your purpose or project. The important thing is to have an easy and clear plan of how you intend to realise it.*

*Be aware that you don't need to put down many details of your goal at this stage, and don't worry if you don't know how to reach it, because now the purpose of the exercise is to write down your goal on paper to prepare a draft of the main steps!*

So, **ALWAYS WRITE YOUR GOAL DOWN!**

| |
|---|
| **Workout 29**                                **Date:**<br>Write a short summary of your goal and put it in your logbook.<br>My goal is:<br><br><br><br><br><br> |

Having defined what you want and after writing it down in your logbook you should consider memorising it by repeating it many times during the day. This will influence your subconscious!

| Workout 30 | Date: |
| --- | --- |
| My sentence to be repeated every day about my goal is: | |

I personally do this repetition many times during the day and I can tell you that this exercise is very powerful, especially when you decide to go ahead on your road to success or when you want to overcome procrastination. In fact, the purpose of this exercise is to influence your subconscious which will push you to be more effective with enormous benefits to your choices and actions. You will see this change in action because you will have the power to drive yourself where you want to go.

**Remember:** this exercise has the power to allow you to be focused and determined throughout your journey until you reach your aim. I wish to invite you to try it today. Also, repeat your goal out loud - but only when nobody else is there!

## HOW CAN I SET MY GOALS?

First you read important information to understand what a goal really is and how it is different from a desire or a dream. The next workouts will help you to realise your goal and what you really want right now. So, it is your turn!

| Workout 31 | Date: |
|---|---|

Check if your goal has the following characteristics in the boxes, and describe why your goal has these characteristics:

| PERSONAL | CHALLENGING |
|---|---|
| CLEAR | DETAILED |
| ORGANISED into SUB-GOALS | Note: |

**Workout 32**                                    **Date:**

In this workout you have to tick the characteristics that your own goal must have to be effective:

My goal has to be...

**S**pecific

Significant

Stretching

**M**easurable

Meaningful

Motivational

**A**greed upon

Achievable

Action-oriented

**R**elevant

Result-oriented

Rewarding

In a **T**imeframe

Time-bound

Trackable

Now, describe why your goal has these characteristics:

| SPECIFIC | MEASURABLE |
|---|---|
| ATTAINABLE | REALISTIC |
| TIMELY, with a Timeframe. | Note and consideration: |

**Workout 33**                                    **Date:**

Define if your goal is a Minimal, Transitional or Maximum Goal.

**Workout 34**                                    **Date:**

Start to divide your goal into sub-goals. This will allow you to have a clear idea about which steps are useful during your project. This workout will be useful during your action plan.

Dear friend I want to share a story that may inspire you.

Linda Shrimpton is the author of *Be Happy - A Spiritual Journey Including Insight about ETs and our Future!*

In the beginning she had in mind to write and publish her first book; follow her story:

'At that time I did not know what about. Further on in life I became interested in self-development and spirituality. Having made a lot of notes I realised I had the potential to write a book about what I had learned and discovered, so I did some research on how to write a book. I found a three-month course that gave me an outline on how to organise content and self-publish. Three years after my initial self-publishing, a major self-publishing book company got in touch asking if I had finished my book.

'They were happy to re-publish my book, *Be Happy - A Spiritual Journey Including Insight about ETs and our Future!* They offered a discount which enabled me to afford the self-publishing package which included a website, a YouTube book trailer, a press release and various advertising literature. I paid for this in instalments. They offered me a further year's website hosting for free if I paid the total amount. So I did.

'In the meantime, I joined various Meetup groups connected with the subjects I wrote about. Among the groups I came across friendly, helpful people who offered to help me with computer technology and arranging an author/book day at a local library, and an open day to promote and sell my book at a local spiritual church.

My journey is progressing with momentum in a healthy, happy way. So, have an idea, have intentions, carry them out, expect good connections and your goals can come to fruition. I just took small steps, not necessarily knowing all the steps, and my path became clearer as I took them. I put into practice what I had learned in my journey of self-development and it all went well.'

Linda Shrimpton had her goal clear in her mind and she decided to pursue it without hesitation.

In fact, Linda has followed her vision step by step, learning what was necessary as she went along; she was focused on her goal and she was at the same time brilliant and humble enough to ask others for advice. That decision has allowed to her to reach her dream.

Linda improved her skills (in the Competence Area) and created new relationships by trusting people around her (Relationship Area). Linda was able to impact on her life creating a new way to change her future and make her first book a reality (Autonomy Area).

I am sure that Linda Shrimpton's story can help you to clarify your goal and how to achieve it with the same determination.

# WHAT CAN BLOCK YOU ON THIS STEP?

In this part of your project the dangers are multiple and with different origins; luckily, we can overcome them by using care and paying attention.

The next list gives you an idea of the dangers you might encounter along the way:

- Not having a CLEAR GOAL.

- Setting too many goals!

- Over-ambitious goals, without adequate preparation or skills.

- Not changing your strategy at times when needed.

- Judging yourself or your project too severely.

DESCRIBE WHAT CAN BLOCK YOU ON THIS STEP:

## THE THIRD STEP.

WHY?

**Why do you want to achieve your goal?**

*'The greatest enemy of knowledge is not ignorance*
*It is the illusion of knowledge.'*

*Stephen Hawking*

## CLEAR VISION = CLEAR MISSION

*Knowing what you want and why you want to get your goal are the pillars in achieving success in your life.*

Understanding which way to take, even if in part unknown, is essential in taking the first steps towards your goal; having a clear idea in your mind, you will gain the right mindset, confidence and motivation.

Your vision about the future you want will make all the difference! Analysing some aspects of yourself and the goal you want to achieve builds a more complete vision, which you can take inspiration from, now and in the future.

Think about what kind of life famous people would have had if they didn't have clear ideas or a clear vision of their future. Most likely we would not today have **Apple, Facebook, Amazon** or even the invention of **Edison's** light bulb. We have to be grateful to Bell and Meucci for their telephonic inventions, as well as the work on the telegraph and radio transmission by Morse and Marconi.

I want to mention the strength and the tenacity of women in the distant past and recent history who have fought to create a better world even at the price of their own lives, women such as Hypatia in ancient Greece, or Madame Marie Curie or Amelia Earhart who was a pioneer of flight, the first woman to cross the Atlantic solo and the first person to have flown across both the Atlantic and the Pacific. I want to mention Rebecca Stephens, the first British woman to have reached the summit of Mount Everest and the Seven Summits, who inspired the young British woman Bonita Norris to climb Everest at the age of twenty-two!

What kind of world would it be without these lives and without their vision which has improved and changed our existence?

It is vital to have a vision of the future because without it is like driving a car on an unknown road in the darkness; would you drive without knowing where your destination is? So, it is much better to have a clear idea where you want to go.

Is having a clear vision great? Yes, but it isn't enough!

*Your vision defines your future. It must be in line with your values and interests, and your vision will lead your mission.*

**Remember:** you can identify your vision with your orientation, however, the mission relates to the actions you will take over time while your vision could go further.

*The mission is the way to make your vision possible and real!*

I would like to tell you about the great and profound experience of a friend of mine I met during my professional Life Coaching course in Milan. Among the many stories of human lives heard during my days spent with my life coach friends, one of them surprised me. You will also discover, reading later, the value of believing in your dreams and achieving the impossible.

Alberto is the name of a person who taught me not to give in to the difficulties of life but to become stronger than our adversity, fighting to the end for the things which are of real value in life. Alberto is a man of infinite humanity who has lived through the bitter experience of being fired at fifty years old. Maybe you'll think that you know people who have the same problem and you will be wondering what's extraordinary about this? Alberto spent his whole life in the sales department of an important Italian company and one day he was called by the H.R. office with the sad news that he would have to give up his job; for Alberto it's the end. He was fired.

For Alberto came bewilderment, anger, fear, uncertainty. His sadness was amplified by losing an important role in his life after years of dedication and sacrifice. Alberto wondered what the future could give him at his age. After losing his job he felt that he had even lost himself.

His long walks in the vineyards of the beautiful hills of Alba in western Piedmont helped him to reflect and reach the right serenity to find answers again. Alberto understood that he had to start from himself, enhancing his human qualities, his abilities, and above all rediscovering that he had left aside for many years the dream of creating his own perfumes.

And in just one of the phrases heard in Alberto's speeches I found the inspiration to do the impossible and to start from scratch, to create a new life. As Alberto said, 'Dreams are what make us unique, and our uniqueness is our true treasure.'

Alberto, confident in his abilities and with a great desire to realise himself, did not lose heart. After the Life Coaching course he decided to write his book where he tells his life story and how he managed to turn a dark and difficult moment for into a revenge on life. Maybe I was one of the first to read his book *Fired at Fifty Years Old* and I'm still tied to his story, so much so that after more than four years I still feel inspired by it.

In 2012 on his birthday, Alberto created Acqua delle Langhe,(www.acquadellelanghe.it.) a brand that produces artistic perfumes that originate in the Piedmontese Langhe, a geographical area which in June 2014 was even declared a UNESCO World Heritage Site. It is the scents of his landscape that inspired the fragrances of his first three perfumes.

I am amazed by the perseverance and courage of Alberto and I never cease to amaze myself. He creates his famous essences that are now available in Russia, Slovakia, United Arab Emirates, Israel, Costa Rica, Brazil, South Africa, Germany and Norway. I would say not bad for a man left without work at fifty!

I have not seen Alberto for years but I can say, dear friend, that I will always be grateful to Alberto Avetta, a great man who with his tenacity, perseverance, instinct and a good idea was activated to create a new life, even better than the one before. And if he could do it and I'm doing it myself, I think anyone can do it.

I hope that the Alberto Avetta could be helpful to you so you can find ideas and motivation during your goal, but what made the difference in Alberto's experience?

Definitely a clear vision and profound sense of mission that were made possible by a great decision.

# CLEAR DECISION.

Your vision and mission are achievable only with a clear and well-defined decision. Your decision and your choices can help you to become free and independent (Autonomy Area), having the necessary skills or learning new ones (Competence Area).

Above all, you will be ready for the countless opportunities presented to you by creating connections with new people (Relationship Area).

*'There are no good or bad decisions but there are only different results.'*

*Cristian Cairo*

Only you can give meaning to the results you obtain in accordance with your expectations. You must not feel down or confused when you make decisions, but you have to learn to wait for the results of your choices and actions. In fact, one of the ways to approach your expectations about your decisions is to take control of your actions creating the necessary conditions for your goal.

Making decisions is never easy but you can train yourself a little at a time and manage the stress better. Train yourself to make decisions even when you do not want to, because this is the only way to take control of your life.

*'It doesn't matter what you decide now but it is important that you decide!'*

## DISCOVERING THE MEANING BEHIND YOUR GOAL.

*Your reasons are important because they are like a light in the darkness; knowing your own reasons is the best way to know yourself and you can train yourself to stay motivated along your road to success, looking at the reasons that drive you to act every day.*

## YOUR MANIFESTO!

**Workout 35**                                        **Date**

# WHY ARE YOU TAKING YOUR ROAD TO SUCCESS?

Write down the reasons why you want to achieve your goal and identify the purpose that drives you.

Your Vision:

Your Mission in your life:

My Mission related to my goal:

# VALUES AND GOALS

*'He who knows others is wise; he who knows himself is enlightened.'*

*Lao-Tzu*

The goals that are linked to your values are more achievable. Indeed, a goal linked with your values creates a strong motivation that gives you more satisfaction. During the Via on Character and Strengths test you came to know yourself better and you have seen how your strengths can make the difference, especially when they are connected to your values.

**Remember:** if your goal isn't linked to your values, it gives you weak or no motivation; in fact, you risk your goal not being achieved at all, or you could experience a lack of satisfaction when you do achieve it.

Rather it is better to give up, finding other solutions or pursuing your goal at other times; for example, should you give in to your family for a job promotion abroad? Perhaps, but it is much better to think properly about the future consequences and their impact on your relationships. Instead, if your decision can give important benefics to you and your family, you could start to think of working abroad, living far away from your family for a time. In this example you can see how three important areas in your life may not be matched with your personal values, the areas in this case are Competencies, Relationship and Autonomy; if you aren't able to satisfy at least one of these areas you can end up demotivated. When your goals don't reflect your values this can generate stress, sadness and decline in performance as well as a future disinterest in the goal itself. This situation is experienced strongly by those who live a life decided by other people or events.

Through the Wheel of Life you can understand when your values are not expressed or not respected by yourself, thus supporting the compromises that occur in life which cause dissatisfaction over time and poor consideration of what is important to us, leading to unhappiness and disappointment.

At times, however, some compromise of our values may be necessary for a while.

---

**Workout 36**                                    **Date:**

Try to think of the last time that you accomplished something and you felt very happy.

---

Describe the feelings that you experienced in that moment.

Describe the personal values that are linked with your goal.

**Workout 37**                                    **Date:**

Make a list of the values that you would never give up in life.

Think of those values that distinguish you as a person.

**Workout 38**                                    **Date:**

Identify in which areas of the Wheel of Life you are doing or could do things against your values.

*I am ready to give up certain values, especially temporarily if...*

## FIND YOUR MOTIVATIONS.

Having written the reasons why you want to take the road to success, find the motivation that will guide you on your pathway; a sole motivator can make the difference! Think how many times as a child you insisted on returning to the theme park because you experienced beautiful emotions that gave you the determination to insist on going back there; you had a good reason to go back... because it was fun! Around us we have wonderful examples of many people who work as volunteers, as well as many professionals who work seriously to give their best to their customers; all these people have one or more motivators that drive them to live extraordinary lives. Now it's your turn!

**Remember:** *Your Motivators will remind you of what leads you to reach for your goal and they are useful in helping you find determination.*

**Workout 39**                    **Date:**

Identify what motivates you and write down your main motivators. (*You could do this workout with a partner so you can find something in common that will drive both of you every day.*)

## INTERNAL AND EXTERNAL MOTIVATORS.

Now you know your own motivations, but do you know how they can impact on your life?

How do you know that your motivations will drive you to your goal?

Julian Rotter formulated his theory called *the locus of control*, which explains clearly that the outcomes of our actions and behaviours are connected to our personal characteristics.

Do you remember the sentences I wrote: as you think, you act?

Well, Julian Rotter in his studies discovered that we have two kinds of locus of control:

- the internal locus of control

- and the external locus of control

The people with an internal locus of control are more successful, in fact they know how to manage their skills and raise their performance. They are able to delay small gratifications with enormous advantages to their motivation. If you believe that with your mindset and your actions it is possible to lead your life well, it is because you have this kind of locus.

On the other hand, if you strongly need someone else's support, advice and encouragement, it is because you have an external locus of control.

Understanding the difference between the two types of locus can help you to know your personal attitudes, how you can take control of the environment around you, and how you respond to certain stimuli in the environment.

From researchers' studies we know that successful people can stay on their road to success because they have learned or developed their internal locus of control, which allows them to overcome their procrastination, becoming more confident in making decisions.

Which are the motivators that lead people in their decisions?

With **External Motivators** you can act to accomplish something because you need others' approval or external awards. I suggest using this kind of motivator to drive you to a short-term goal where it will be easy to achieve sub-goals, rewarding yourself with little prizes.

Instead, with **Internal Motivators** you will challenge yourself according to your own expectation and personal desires. Sometimes, in fact, you may act because you have identified your reasons with situations in the external environment. For instance, you may join a peace march because it is linked to your own feelings and motivations.

The next workout can help you to evaluate your internal or external locus of control, clarifying your self-doubts and focusing on your real motivation to persevere in your goal.

**Workout 40**                                    **Date:**

## The Question of your Destiny.

- Is the challenge really IMPORTANT to me?




- Am I confident enough to achieve my goal?

- What can I do when I feel that I can't control something in my project?

- Do I have the TIME to be committed to plan, prepare and deliver my own CHALLENGE?

- Do I have the RESOURCES for my CHALLENGE?

- Am I able to persevere in my plan without others' approval?

- What kind of prize can I reward myself in achieving a sub-goal?

## MY PERSONAL STATEMENT OF ACHIEVEMENT.

Usually I advise my clients to make their own statement of achievement because it allows them to record their promises and keep track of their improvements and be responsible for their goals.

With your personal statement of achievement, it is possible to sign a commitment to yourself, with a precise date, that makes you responsible and which you will use as a reference, to check if your promise is kept.

Another person witnessing this will strengthen your commitment and, moreover, the engagement of that person will help you to receive feedback and advice. It would be a good idea to do this type of contract with a coach, a mentor or tutor who can help you achieve your goals.

By making a formal commitment to your goal and when you will achieve it, you will be more successful!

**Workout 41**                                    **Date:**

*My proposal is:*

.

*I promise that:*

 Name:

Signed:

 Witness/Tutor/Coach

 Date:

## WHAT CAN BLOCK YOU ON THIS STEP?

Your Beliefs.

Your poor Commitment.

Your poor Motivation.

Your poor Determination.

Your poor Actions.

Describe what can block you and how you want to solve it:

# THE FOURTH STEP.

## WHO?

*'People who are unable to motivate themselves must be content with mediocrity, no matter how impressive their other talents.'*
*Andrew Carnegie*

**Who is the protagonist of your story, your challenge and your dream?**

Is it you? Or is it those who try to show you the way, suggesting what is best for you or what you could do in life? Suggestions as well as advice are always pleasant to receive, especially from people who love us and those who express a genuine intention of helping us to choose what to do in the future. But sometimes it happens that we feel oppressed, submissive, useless or worthless, because certain people around us, with their judgements and unhelpful feedback, can 'manipulate' our destiny. When you feel yourself in these situations, you would like to change everything and struggle to find yourself, rediscovering your true nature, even at the cost of finding yourself isolated from the people around you.

Read books that can help you to understand your past and current relationships and how to develop your assertive communication skills, especially in your workplace or with family. In this way you can learn how to have good partnerships and how to manage conflicts that are sometimes unavoidable.

Try to think in a win-win mode. This can be another good piece of advice to manage your self-esteem and your relationships better; in fact, it can allow you to create good relationships and avoid hurting people by your reactions.

**Create good feeling with the people around you.**

Lear to synergise! Achieving your goal alone is almost impossible. In any case you need to ask others, asking advice from experts, who will give you another point of view based on their experience and above all on their own results.

As Napoleon Hill wrote in his book *The Law of Success*, a master mind is the alliance of two minds joining in a harmonious way. This means that all of us need to create relationships at every level in our society and environment. By making relationships we have the power to form new ideas and a new vision in way that is profitable for all the partners involved.

Think about your goal: it will be impossible to achieve it only with your own energy and competences. Working together in co-operation is more powerful than working alone. See the power of networking, surrounding yourself with other people who are successful or want to succeed, because they have the habit of surrounding themselves with great people too. Building relationships like that is an opportunity to develop quickly yourself, finding the right nurture for your project or idea.

**Remember:** It is important to clarify your intentions so as to prepare people around you for your change, allowing them to share in your new challenge.

The following list will help you to identify what categories of people you could refer to for your problems, ideas, project and life purpose.

In the list I have also included the family and people close to you. Here is a list of people or communities of people you could contact:

- New people around you.

- People or communities of people with a similar goal to yours.

- People who have achieved a goal in your area of interest, to ask for advice, feedback and suggestions.

- Experts in your area.

- Role models from the past and the present.

- Mentors, Coaches and Tutors.

- Your family.

- Your close friends and other relationships.

**Workout  42**                                    **Date:**

Create  your  own  list  of  people  to  ask  for  advice  or opinions

# PAST VS. FUTURE

When you desire something say to yourself, 'Well, the time has come to act!' Energy pervades you and you begin to engage enthusiastically in the new challenge that you have just accepted. But after a few months the dark clouds of doubt and discontent arrive. Why is this? Have you lost enthusiasm and motivation or changed your mind? Analyse each possibility step by step. If we get something wrong we are disappointed and we are full of guilt, often unjustified; this is the moment to stop and reflect on what is happening and pay attention to the thoughts and actions that have created barriers between us and our desired goal.

We can look at our past, analysing the variables and conditions that could have led us to desist on realising our dream. What we are, our thoughts and actions, create the life that we live every day; thoughts influence our actions which in turn will influence our thoughts and especially our belief system and values. Sometimes our opinions and beliefs aren't connected to our external reality, your inner reality is made up of your past experiences, the emotions you have experienced, your beliefs and your personal values - which guide you in your actions in what you believe about yourself and the world around you. Meanwhile, the external reality is the true objective reality with its laws, with its order, and with its organisational systems.

If your internal reality doesn't coincide with the external reality, it could create different ways of responding to events. On the one hand for instance, with confusion or frustration when you don't know the way to solve some problems. On the other hand, if you know what is happening, to a sense of challenge and taking responsibility, becoming the master of your thoughts about the reality in which you live.

## LEARN TO DISCOVER A NEW POINT OF VIEW.

Discovering our point of view and understanding how close it is to reality is a fundamental step for anyone who wishes to live their life with awareness.

Becoming skilled in analysing your past and your current situation will give you the benefit of creating your own point of view. A good exercise is to try, whenever you have the opportunity, to 'change position' in a dialogue.

'Changing position' means trying to identify with other people, their thinking and their point of view. Imagine being the person next to you; the purpose of this exercise is to allow you to create more than one point of view about people, events or a story or news article that you are reading. In practice, the exercise helps you to observe yourself and how you react to the actions of others. Moreover, by placing yourself in another point of view, you can manage certain difficult situations between you and others better.

So, try to change your point of view...

264

| | |
|---|---|
| **YOU** | |
| **SHE/HE** | **WE** |

In a hypothetical three-way dialogue in which you take part (YOU), you could firstly create your own point of view, memorising the important facts about the people present. Then empathising in the second position (SHE/HE) you could get an idea of the possible reasons, motivations and reactions of that person. While in the third position (WE), you would have an overview on the facts given and the possible alternatives that other people have not thought about. The exercise is also useful in developing empathy towards other people, allowing you to compare your point of view with the others present, trying not to make hasty judgements but having an overview of the event.

Another purpose of the exercise is to enable you to have an open mind.

- Keep a record of your experiences with this exercise and review them after a few months, noting if, in the meantime, your style of thinking and your opinion about the people you met has changed.

I gained a lot of interesting advice from Dale Carnegie's bestselling book *How to Win Friends and Influence People* and I invite you to read it, and to give the same opportunity to others you love.

**Your opinions and personal judgements**.

As you have just read, having an open mind will help you both in interpersonal relationships and in keeping your mind ready for the many opportunities that will arise in your life. Do not judge yourself, and try as much as possible to find evidence from the reality which you live in.

*Distinguish the facts from your personal judgements and try to understand how much your comfort zone keeps you imprisoned in old mental schemes that don't allow you to progress.*

Sometimes we could have several different views or opinions about the same situation.

For example, our boss gives us a lot of work to do, some of it quite difficult. One person might see it this way: 'My boss doesn't like me and is trying to pressure me', or 'He thinks I am lazy and wants me to work harder.'

Or another person might judge the situation like this: 'My boss thinks I am a good worker so he can depend on me and he wants me to learn all kinds of tasks.'

**Workout 43**                                    **Date:**

Ask yourself how much your opinions could hinder you on your path of personal growth and in your interpersonal relationships. Write your impressions in your logbook and compare them with another person who can give you their feedback.

**The personal belief of always being right.**

In our lives we have lost more than one opportunity or more than one friendship because of our 'right to always be right'.

I would like to give you an example: suppose you have a job interview and the interviewer asks you about his company.

Maybe you think or suppose you know everything about that company because you have prepared yourself at home, but your pride leads you to give the wrong answer to a specific question, confusing the successes of another company with that of the interviewer. It could be trivial and it isn't; many companies care about their successes and defend them. Let's go on with your hypothetical interview:

The interviewer, although disconcerted, gives you another chance despite having warned you about your wrong answer. In the meantime your pride leads you to insist that you are right. What do you think will happen?

269

This type of situation is quite frequent and not only during a job interview. It happens frequently in discussions between friends, relatives, parents and children. Sometimes being sure of being right and insisting on maintaining this position, even with emotional detachment and empathy towards your interlocutor, leads you to sound defeats and unexpected consequences.

The important thing is not to enter into the area of submission, always giving the reasons to others. It is better to maintain an assertive and empathetic position with the other person, helping you to compare your opinion with theirs.

The ideal is not to oppose the person for his ideas and opinions but to turn your attention to the topic of discussion so that you can argue by showing your opinions constructively with respect and firmness.

- Try to remember the last time that, during a bitter discussion, you lost control or were simply right without trying to argue your ideas.

- What would you have wanted to say, what would you have wanted to avoid saying, and what would you do today if you were in another similar situation?

- Analyse what you think about yourself, your opinions and actions, and ask if you have wasted time, opportunities and friendships because of your stubbornness.

**Workout 44**                                    **Date:**

Write down what, how and why you would like to
change some negative aspects of your character:

**The future.**

Analysing the negative aspects that could hinder you will help you pay attention to future events, especially when those events could affect your determination, your motivation and your effectiveness in achieving your goal. Being prepared and ready to react positively will allow you to stay focused on your strengths and your abilities, reviewing the goals achieved in the meantime.

You must stay focused on these:

- Your goal, which in part represents what you want for your future.

- The actions that need to be done progressively and maintained over time, respecting yourself by not overloading your commitments.

- Act with a plan and a purpose that motivates you more and more, giving you confidence and personal pride.

- Have a new and constructive point of view which will allow you to grow as a person as well as open the doors to new opportunities and relationships.

## CHANGE YOUR MINDSET

*Think how your past can block you in creating your future goal.*

Evaluate your mind: if you don't think but just act what are the consequences? Think before you act.

Having your own point of view shows that you have ideas regarding life. Sometimes your old point of view could damage your present and your future. Try to develop a new point of view.

Try to remember the last time your reaction drove you into making mistakes. Maybe you reacted because you were stubborn or because you didn't care about others' opinions. Try to change your opinion and think of giving others the opportunity to express their ideas.

*Don't always decide alone but try to ask others' opinions.*

Do you know the difference between force and power? *With power you can act through your strengths; instead, with only force, you just act without making any impact on your life or action plan.*

Evaluate if complaining about people or events around you has impacted negatively on your life. Maybe it is time to change your mindset and be more committed to your plans. Be careful how you think: excuses and indecision have consequences for your future so try to imagine if you had been more open minded in the past what you could have achieved today.

Examine why you are still in your *comfort zone.* Step by step you can learn *self-determination* in your life through slow improvement and evaluating the change in yourself honestly.

# THE FOUNDATION OF ACCEPTANCE.

In the Autonomy area you saw that if you want to be free to determine your pathway you need to understand who you are. That is one of the most important steps if you want to improve or change your current situation. First of all you need to accept who you are, then you can learn how to become the person that you want to be and not a copy of someone else. If you are autonomous you can have the power that allows you to decide what you need and want and to achieve things in your own way.

**Remember:** develop your strengths instead of just accepting your weakness or changing yourself to be accepted by others around you. In the same way it is much better to take control of the circumstances and events around you instead of burning your energy trying to change them.

I want to show you four elements that you can use in your self-acceptance. These are steps that allow you to consider yourself in a different way, as described by the psychologist Marsha Linehan.

1) Accept yourself and the situations around you with knowledge about their origins and nature; accept the fact that they are just events and circumstances.

2) Don't judge yourself and the situation around you but try to evaluate them, taking a different approach that allows you to experience positive learning.

3) Don't resist your sufferings but allow to them to go away.

4) Accept that all things go away if you see them as something that just happens in your life.

**Workout 45**                                    **Date:**

Describe how you are living at the present time, trying to accept the circumstances around you. Then describe what you should change to manage the present time with a new approach.

# WHAT IS RESILIENCE?

We can speak of resilience in engineering and metallurgy, meaning the ability of a material to resist shocks without breaking, while in biology we are in the presence of resilient organisms when they are able to repair themselves after suffering damage.

As you have guessed resilience is the ability to resist without being overpowered by difficulties, by adapting to different situations.

The same thing happens to human beings; in fact, in psychology resilience indicates the ability to resist, facing and reorganising your own life, while we are living through or have experienced a negative event.

The resilient individual is one who manages to move forward, aware of his inner power (or discovering that he has it), developing a deeper self-awareness. Those who are resilient don't hide behind problems ignoring reality or deny the difficulties they have to deal with.

The resilient person succeeds in transforming a problem into a learning opportunity understood as the ability to acquire skills and knowledge useful to overcome difficulties, thus improving one's quality of life by continuing one's own path of growth and fulfilment.

There are individual and social characteristics that make a resilient type of response more likely. Surely being positive and optimistic is one of the important features that make the difference, but it is also true that this should not be confused with the temptation to belittle problems, rather it is the capacity to accept problems which are an inevitable component of life.

The difficulties must be considered:

- transitory.

- non-permanent.

- circumscribed.

- not always dependent on you and you may not be responsible for them.

- an interaction of several factors, some of which are beyond your control.

It is important to note that the human environment around us is a determining factor in whether resources are developed to face difficulties.

A positive input and atmosphere can nourish us. On the other hand a negative human influence will not allow us to express ourselves or use our strength to face problems or difficulties.

Both self-esteem and self-efficacy are two of the countless resources we have with which to overcome the problems and negative events of life. They make a resilient response more likely if they are developed in an appropriate environment. But at the same time it is our response to the different situations that makes the difference, and this is often nothing to do with the environment in which we live - as with many examples of people you will read about in this book.

Those who value themselves on a personal level can develop the ability to cope with the difficulties they encounter. Being confident of their resources and skills, they will be resilient despite the environment in which they live.

**How can resilience be developed or improved?**

Surely the ability to tolerate frustration and stress also allows you to metabolise discomforts, defeats and fatigue, as happened to me during the writing of my book where I had to stay focused for a long time under stress, trying to ward off the mirages of success and the small gratifications that could reward me without giving me what I was looking for.

In fact, I once again developed the capacity to defer the gratification of the present moment to pursue and persevere in achieving my goal of finishing the book within a month.

The thoughtful choice of having a clear, specific, personal and above all realistic goal was fundamental, at the same time motivating and not too stressful as I had planned to write every day at least two hours.

As my dad Mario taught me since my childhood, it is important to develop humour that should not be seen as a disinterest or trivialisation of problems, but rather as considering events from multiple perspectives and learning to look at them from a distance. From there we can have a global vision of the problems and their nature and above all of the resources to be used to overcome them.

Humour is useful because it represents a functional response to stress. In fact, it reduces its negative impact, producing endorphins and catecholamines.

Furthermore, humour when used intelligently can be a trump card to dampen tensions in a group of people, making sure that a difficult situation can change for the better for everyone present.

Resilience can be developed in all environmental and human conditions, and it can also improve over time using the numerous workouts proposed in this book, among these the strengths and virtues test and the questions on talent will contribute to your ability to be resilient.

First of all it is important to evaluate how we see the world around us. That is the way that an individual conceptualises and explains the events that happen and what he/she sees can affect his or her life.

Changing your beliefs and thought patterns are essential steps to fortify one's resilience. In fact it is not possible to develop this ability without changing your mind and beliefs about your personal skills and the world.

**Remember:** the resilient person does not ignore or avoid suffering.

The resilient person is aware of being able to modify events and how they can affect them on an emotional level, adopting specific models of thought that will help them to consider the problems as well as events that occur, then using their resources to address them without self-judgement if it happens to fail.

*The resilient person is one who looks to past adversities and defeats as a useful lesson to improve oneself and not to repeat the same mistakes by following the same thought patterns; indeed, the resilient person wants to get out of his comfort zone to develop in order to open up to a world full of opportunities.*

What can help you to develop resilience?

Those who want to be resilient must train their ability to be flexible in their choices and decisions and with the people around them. This exercise will be useful to measure your ability to adapt in every situation and with every type of person you will meet.

*Do something different. Do something that involves meeting new people or being in an unfamiliar environment.*

**Workout 46**                                        **Date:**

- Make at first an analysis about your emotions and think how it can influence your choices.

- Then think how you can get out from your comfort zone and drive yourself to do something new.

- Reflect on your resources and abilities that you have developed or used during your resilience workout.

- Express how these resources of yours will be useful in the future, especially in cases of difficulties or problems:

## WHAT CAN BLOCK YOU ON THIS STEP?

- Your poor attitude.

- your reasons.

- your excuses.

- your justifications.

- your feelings connected to your false beliefs.

Describe WHAT CAN BLOCK YOU ON THIS STEP and work out the options to allow you to find the solutions.

# THE FIFTH STEP.

## HOW?

'Faith is taking the first step even when you don't see the whole staircase.'

Martin Luther King

# HOW DO YOU THINK YOU WANT ACHIEVE YOUR GOAL?

**Workout 47**                                    **Date:**

Think about the process of reaching your goal. How will you approach it? What will you do? Write down your ideas without judging them (good or bad). Take all the time you need.

# THE WALT DISNEY MODEL.

During a business coaching session with Jose Luis Ucar La Salvia, the Finding Excellence founder, my weakness emerged. I couldn't implement a real business plan regarding my book. Even though I was used to managing my action plans and helping my clients do the same, this time it was different.

I had to rely on Jose's experience in order to analyse my ability to engage in self-criticism, putting aside the excitement of selling my book right away and preparing myself adequately towards my final goal without risking losing my motivation. Jose told me what the reason for my weakness was. Despite having always been realistic in my life, I had to learn how to be **critical** regarding certain aspects of the book and the marketing strategies.

In fact I was so immersed in my dream that I had forgotten to concentrate on the most concrete aspects such as creating a marketing plan commensurate with my abilities, my financial resources and my expectation regarding future book sales. It was time to be critical about the whole project of the book. As Jose also explained to me we all have conversations with ourselves, sometimes they are negative and some are encouraging and motivational. The key is to be able to detect when we are having these conversations and become aware of the impact they are having on our state of mind and our life. I am grateful to Jose because I needed to discover a new way of thinking and to learn to find the right balance between different kinds of thinking patterns that I was using.

Our thinking patterns are like the glasses thorough which we see the world and through which our lives manifest.

So where is the balance? How can we benefit from these different dialogues that we run in our minds?

Depending on the internal dialogue we have, we can become dreamers, critics and realists.

How can we use these characters to achieve our desired life and reach our outcomes?

The answer to this question lies in our ability to consciously switch from one character to another, taking perspectives, learning from each one of them, and applying them to a specific situation.

In fact we have to be aware that to live in Wonderland every single day may not be the answer, just as always being the villain of the story isn't either. On the other hand, if we decide to be realistic all the time it would be pretty boring, wouldn't it? So where is the answer?

The *dreamer* will show you what can be achieved with no limits, *the realiser* will challenge those dreams and finally *the critic,* from a detached out-of-the-equation perspective, will take insights from the two former positions to formulate a more objective view.

Moving through the above characters we can provide additional information and resources that will allow us to overcome challenges and improve our decision making processes.

Specifically, the **Disney Method** is a strategy developed by Robert Dilts in 1994 which describes four thinking styles that we use in different ways to analyse a problem, generate ideas, evaluate ideas, construct and critique a plan of action. These four thinking styles are called: the dreamer, the outsider, the realiser and the critic.

The dreamer is the one who has the power to think creatively like a child without judging his or her own ideas.

The outsider thinks about the dreamer's ideas from an analytical and external view. Meanwhile, the realiser thinks in a pragmatic way: the realiser is a realist who uses convergent thinking to review the ideas imagined by the dreamer. The realiser is able to be focused, select the best idea, and make a plan for it.

The critic reviews the plan made by the realiser in order to identify weaknesses, obstacles or risks, and tries to find new options to improve the plan.

By using these four types of thinking levels we can push on to our goal, allowing our dreamer to think in freedom. After finding a complete overview of our ideas as the outsider, we can start to make an action plan as the realiser, finding many solutions or options.

In the end we can act as a critic to evaluate if our goal is realistic and feasible.

Now you know that your goal can become real because you have a clear goal in mind instead of a mere dream. But how do you know that it can actually be done, assuring its success? After having imagined your goal as a DREAMER, now it is time to look from outside from different points of view as an OUTSIDER. Then think like a REALISER whether your project or goal can objectively be done. Be CRITICAL and analyse your goal, describing any aspects that can be changed to improve it. Do not lose your motivation but consider all aspects as a way of improving your goal with the aim of being able to realise it to the best of your abilities without wasting time and energy.

# USE THE DISNEY MODEL TO ANALYZE YOUR GOAL.

**Workout 48**                                    **Date:**

The Dreamer in me suggested:




The Outsider in me suggested:

The Realiser in me suggested:

The Critic in me suggested:

# What characterises a good action plan?

At first you wrote down your ideas about your goal in line with your core values, then you have seen how to plan considering your skills and your tasks. Now, there is an explanation of how to make a good action plan so that you can rethink and reset it making it more reliable. So what characterises a good action plan?

- A precise purpose.

- A meaning.

- Practical feasibility.

- A run time.

- Personal strengths.

- New places and new people.

- And it has to be satisfying!

I am sure that in your life you have wondered how it is possible for certain kinds of people to be successful; first of all, they have a precise purpose that has to be very clear. Think if Marie Curie the famous Polish physicist and chemist hadn't had a clear goal of understanding radiation, maybe today she wouldn't be remembered for her contribution to the fight against cancer (www.mariecurie.org.uk).

So is it important to have in mind a clear, precise purpose? The answer is yes but you need to clarify what your goal means to you, or better, what the meaning behind your vision is.

Aspiring to do your best to reach your goal, you need to know your personal strengths that can make the difference in your project. You will discover in this book how to manage your time better with a good action plan which is connected to a run time.

**Remember:** all the components of your action plan are equally important, but the most important thing is *the challenge* you set yourself. This gives meaning to your project.

**Workout 49**                                        **Date:**

Be inspired by the goal characteristics. Evaluate if
your goal has the characteristics mentioned above:

## VISUALISE YOUR ACTION PLAN.

The technique of visualisation is an amazing and useful tool to observe your goal in your mind. Now it is time to visualise your action plan!

Find a quiet place to relax yourself for at least an hour so you can visualise your action plan without any disturbance. Please switch off all devices that might distract you and check that nobody is around you.

**Workout 50**                                    **Date:**

- Take a seat and make yourself comfortable.

- be relaxed and control your breathing, inhale deeply counting for up to three seconds then exhale for at least five seconds. Breathe slowly paying attention to how your stomach lifts. The purpose is to learn to breathe from your stomach rather than to use only your diaphragm. Do this exercise for at least two minutes.

- When you feel relaxed enough be focused, recall

your goal to mind and create your action plan for it in a slow-motion mode. In this phase it is important to start from the 'already realised goal' then go backwards with the mind up to the individual components. Imagine what to do, the things you will need, the people you will meet and the places you will go.

- Record the emotions and feelings you felt during this workout, trying to understand the reasons that have created them. In addition, pay attention to them because your feelings will drive you in your decisions.

**Workout 51**                                    **Date:**

**Write down your visualised action plan in your logbook.**

- Put together all your ideas in an 'embryonic action plan'.

# MAKE THE DIFFERENCE WITH BRAINSTORMING!

With visualisation you have started to create your embryonic action plan. Now with brainstorming you can put together more ideas and possibilities which you can add to your plan. In this phase you can create a list about your tasks and the equipment that you need with Brainstorming.

**Remember:** think without interruptions and report your ideas in your logbook; don't worry if some of your ideas aren't doable or linked with your goal because you can be inspired from any ideas that come up during this workout.

**Workout 52**                                    **Date:**

Start with your brainstorming, now!

I will give two suggestions:

1) The first one is to write down any ideas in a short time. You can start with ten minutes, then twenty minutes, then thirty minutes so you will feel under pressure and your brain will use both its hemispheres to your great advantage.

2) The second suggestion is to ask others to help you with your brainstorming. They will be free to do their own brainstorming based on your proposal, idea or goal without giving any advice to you. Then you will read their versions where you can get new tips for your action plan.

## THE FOUR Ps.

After having created enough ideas with the Brainstorming workout, it will be useful to write them down in the right order using the Four Ps. This is an easy way to summarise and to keep in order what you need. The origin of the Four Ps is from the theory explained by Jerome McCarthy in *Marketing Mix Management*, and nowadays we have different versions of it like in the following workout.

**Workout 53**                                             **Date:**

## Create your own Four P-list.

In accordance with the Walt Disney Model look at the skills that you have or you have to learn for your goal and the main tasks that you can do now. (You can use one or more pages for this exercise.)

- My Priority skills connected with my project:

- My Priority task:

- My list of the People who can help or support me:

- My Places, where I can meet new people and find information:

# THE S.W.O.T. ANALYSIS

*How discovering opportunities, managing and eliminating barriers to being ready to perform better and faster.*

With the S.W.O.T. analysis you can estimate your own strengths, your weaknesses, your opportunities and the threats related to your action plan, analysing your goal in a strategic way.

By doing this workout you will be able to identify the internal and external factors that can help or be disadvantages to your plan. With the internal factors you can identify your personal strengths that can help you to complete your action plan successfully.

The best use of the S.W.O.T. analysis is to find your strengths that will be matched to the opportunities that you will meet, converting your weaknesses into strengths and the threats into opportunities. Let me give you an example: in my childhood I had a friend who was very tall and skinny. For this reason he was bullied at the school. He didn't have any interests in his spare time apart from his love of studying. Staying alone helped him to focus on his homework. In fact he was a brilliant student and achieved excellent results at school.

In a certain way he was lucky: being alone all the time allowed my friend to find other interests such as sport and handicraft. His father told him that nobody could prevent his happiness and self-development, so he started practising his favourite sport, bodybuilding, at home, making his own equipment for himself. Yes, my friend made his own bodybuilding equipment 'with his own hands'.

He started training every day and within two years he became completely different.

He was so muscular and athletic that no one could remember it was him. So what helped him?

My old friend accepted his condition and did his best to change it.

I think we can change our circumstances if we are able to accept them. Maybe it isn't good to force ourselves to change our lives for others, or indeed for our desire and dreams, but sometimes, as may happen in life, it is the only way to change - pushing ourselves into a challenge that can reveal to us who we really are.

As my old friend, you need to identify your personal and goal weaknesses that can create disadvantages to your project so as to delay or block your action plan.

Accepting this you can prevent any problems during your project and make the necessary improvements to it. Ask yourself questions about the areas that can have a significant impact on your project and try to write down your answer giving you a complete overview of your internal and external strengths or weaknesses.

# The S.W.O.T. analysis scheme.

**Workout 54**                                    **Date:**

| Helpful to your goal | Harmful to your goal |
|---|---|
| Internal | Internal |
| **STRENGHS** | **WEAKNESSES** |
| 1 | 1 |
| 2 | 2 |
| 3 | 3 |
| 4 | 4 |
| 5 | 5 |
| 6 | 6 |
| External | External |
| **OPPORTUNITIES** | **THREATS** |
| 1 | 1 |
| 2 | 2 |
| 3 | 3 |
| 4 | 4 |
| 5 | 5 |
| 6 | 6 |

- How can I use my strengths better for my project?

- How can I transform the project's weaknesses?

- How can I search for the opportunities that my project needs?

- How can I prevent the threats during my project?

# ADVANTAGES AND DISADVANTAGES.

Thinking about the advantages and disadvantages related to your project will help you to have a detailed overview, allowing you to make better decisions and avoid those situations that could be harmful or iniquitous.

*Moreover, having clear advantages and benefits related to your project is a way of increasing your motivation.*

Compile a list of the advantages and disadvantages of achieving your goal, what benefits you could get with it and what you risk by not achieving it.

**Remember**: usually, the benefits are achieved after you have attained your goal, but advantages may be experienced on the path while you are working for your goal.

| ADVANTAGES | DISADVANTAGES |
|---|---|
| BENEFITS | RISKS if I don't achieve my goal |

# IMPACT ACTION PLAN
# OR MASSIVE ACTION PLAN?

*An Impact action plan is something that can make a change in one or two areas of your life and in your current goal.*

When you start drafting your action plan it is important to consider the impact that your actions can have on the goal.

Wondering about the consequences of your goal in the future will allow you to act in one way rather than the other. At the same time, when you set your action plan you have to think how to impact on your reality in a smart way.

For instance, as my English tutor Roy Keene has always recommended to me, if you want to learn a foreign language it is better to attend a language course where you can listen to the pronunciation, repeat sentences with the right structure, memorise new words and have fun meeting new people rather than studying books without practising and making any improvement.

A **Massive Plan** is an action plan that covers more areas in your life or in your business plan. The Massive Action Plan is made up of different Impact Action Plans.

The consequence is that you need to be well prepared, usually for twelve months or more, because it will cover a long period of your life.

Again, the Massive Plan requires you to focus on more areas and it needs strong motivation and determination.

For instance, a Massive Plan is required when a company has to rethink its purpose, or when you need to set an action plan for a long period of time that will cover all three main areas in your life (Competence, Relationships and Autonomy).

*Remember:* sometimes a single Impact Action Plan can give more results than a Massive Action Plan; the only difference is in your strategies.

**Workout 56**                                         **Date:**

-Try to explain to yourself if you need an Impact
Action Plan or Massive Action Plan and why, giving
the consequences, benefits and advantages.


My Impact Plan...

# My Massive Plan...

# YOUR ACTION PLAN
## WITH THE EISENHOWER METHOD.

After you have decided what your priorities are, it is time to give each one the right importance, so you can do your tasks faster and better getting the advantage of an ordered list. (You could use your FOUR P. LIST for this workout, for instance.)

1) Think about your priorities.

2) Make your list.

3) Decide which of your priorities have to be in A, B, C, D or E.

A = it is a very important task with serious consequences!

It is something that YOU MUST DO NOW!

B = a task that you should do. B has only moderate consequences and it isn't urgent.

C = something that doesn't have consequences for your life or priority goal.

D = something that is not important that you can delegate to someone else.

E = it is a task that you can ELIMINATE from your task list.

**Remember:** don't go on to the next task if you haven't completed your current tasks; e.g. If you are involved in A, don't start doing tasks in B!

# Workout 57    YOUR DAILY TASKS          Date:

(You can make a table like this every day)

| A tasks:<br>1<br>2<br>3<br>4<br>5<br>**DO IT NOW!** | B tasks:<br>1<br>2<br>3<br>4<br>5<br>**IT ISN'T URGENT.** |
|---|---|
| D tasks:<br>1<br>2<br>3<br>4<br>5<br>**Delegate!** | C tasks:<br>1<br>2<br>3<br>4<br>5<br>**Ignore at the moment!** |

| E tasks:<br><br>**Eliminate!** |
|---|

## WHAT CAN BLOCK YOU ON THIS STEP?

### YOUR HABITS!

Yes, your habits can block you on the road to success... but fortunately you can create positive habits that will drive you to a rich and meaningful life. Discover how your habits can impact on your personal development.

### POSITIVE HABITS = POSITIVE TRAINING

### NEGATIVE HABITS = NEGATIVE TRAINING

*'Success is the product of daily habits, not once-in-a-lifetime transformations.'*

*James Clear*

Your bad habits don't change without a strong purpose that can lead you into new positive habits; learn how to create your own system that can allow you to change your bad habits into good habits. In fact, new habits will be powerful if they make a permanent change in your life and this is possible with a strong system. This system must be repeatable and you have to see your change with small steps, finding a good balance between what you are ready to give up and how much you are willing to change your bad habits.

Allow yourself to change your old habits in a progressive and natural way little by little, introducing small improvements over a period of time.

Consider that your new habits will shape your identity through a process that requires time. Change what you are doing that can stop you becoming the person you want to be with new small tasks every day.

Successful people are able to stay on the road to success because they maintain daily practices and tasks that are useful to their goals. They have developed the right mindset, and you can copy their behaviours such as:

- Begin with the end in mind: as you read before, it is useful to start from the end of your project so you can have a clear vision of it.

- Stay on track with passion, and don't allow yourself to lose your motivation.

- Put first things first. After you have set your goal, you have to stay committed until your project is completed.

- Create a strong action plan: invest your energy and time into all the details that can impact on it.

- Trust yourself and believe in yourself.

- Be responsible and take control of your life.

- Take risks.

- Follow your instincts. Be aware of what your body and your mind want to tell you. If necessary, allow yourself to have a good rest and recharge; restart well energised!

- Learn from your mistakes and how to avoid certain strategies that are unproductive, learning to consider ideas that you didn't think of before.

- Be positive. This means having the right mindset without following illusions.

I want to share with you other suggestions from the worldwide bestseller *The 7 Habits of Highly Effective People* by one of my favourite authors, Stephen R. Covey.

According to Steve Covey if you want to be successful you need to follow your principles, and at the same time you have to attend to your needs, desires, priorities and goals, getting the right balance between your final goal and your ability to reach it. Use your strengths, your skills and your motivation to boost your results towards your goal. But you have to be aware of how you see yourself and the world around you.

As you have learned in this book your character is formed by your main beliefs, strengths, actions and habits, and habits play an important role in your life. What does the word 'habit' mean? It consists of a settled or regular tendency or practice, especially one that is hard to give up including behaviours that can impact negatively on our lives.

Stephen R. Covey explained clearly that habits affect our decisions, so how can we change our mindset?

Covey's focus is centred on self-mastery: if you want to achieve victories it is necessary to move from dependence to independence and to develop the habit to being fully committed, showing your personal capability and making the difference between your current and future life.

**Workout 58**                                    **Date:**

## My habits.

| My positive habits: | My negative habits: |
|---|---|
|  |  |
|  |  |
|  |  |
|  |  |
|  |  |
|  |  |
|  |  |
|  |  |
|  |  |
|  |  |
|  |  |

I can transform my negative habits if...

My negative habits that I couldn't give up...!

Which new actions can I do to build new solid and positive habits?

Choose three habits that you want to change:

1-

2-

3-

Now, create your new daily habits with a week schedule so you can monitor your progress. Use your logbook or a diary.

## THE SIXTH STEP

IDENTIFY YOUR FACTORS OF SUCCESS!

*'Live as if you were to die tomorrow. Learn as if you were to live forever.'*

*Mahatma Gandhi*

Maybe in the past you have asked yourself the following question: why are certain people able to accomplish their goal? We know that words like persistence, courage, preparation, determination, time management and self-control are usually what we use to describe successful people's characteristics, but there is something more - the **Factors of Success**!

*The Factors of Success make the difference in your goal: if you want to succeed you must be effective through those elements that allow you to achieve your goal.*

For instance: two cyclists took part in a cycling competition and one of them won it. They had the same trainer, the same kind of bicycle and the same health status. Why did one of them win?

The answer is that one of them had made excellent and accurate *preparation* with his *equipment!* He has monitored each component of his equipment, forecasting any risks during the competition, and has successfully prevented delays and annoyances that could jeopardise his race.

In the same way you can monitor in every detail the strategic areas of your goal that will require to be developed, evaluating which of them can impact positively on your action plan.

I have identified two categories of Factors of Success. They are:

- Primary Factors of Success

- Secondary Factors of Success

The Primary Factors of Success are connected to your own preparation, skills, competence, education and knowledge that can be developed with appropriate training and effort.

*The Primary Factors of Success are personal characteristics that allow you to start on your project: you know what you can do and you can always improve these personal characteristics during the execution of your plan.*

*The Secondary Factors of Success* are related to the specific nature of your goal and if you want to succeed or make a difference in your field. You need to stay focused on the characteristics that allow you to emerge among your main competitors. If you have a personal goal you can also apply the concept of the Secondary Factors of Success to your project. Look to the next workout so you can evaluate how it can work for you and which of them can make a significant impact and an improvement in your action plan. Think calmly and pay attention to the Factors of Success that need to be developed.

After a period of three months it will be fine to monitor how your Factors of Success have worked; consider changing them if they aren't relevant to your project.

**Workout 59**                                        **Date:**

**Give a score to your Factors of Success from 0 to 10.**

The Primary Factors of Success:

- Your VISION about your Goal.

- Your Motivation.

- Your Persistence.

- Your Strengths in your Area.

- Your Skills.

- Your Education and Knowledge.

- Your Competence related to your Project.

The Secondary Factors of Success:

- Your detailed Action Plan.

- Your Time Management skill.

- Your Tasks.

- Your Equipment.

- Your Financial situation.

- Your Expert.

- Your Environment.

This list is just an example to help simplify my explanation about the Factors of Success. You can create your own list, and it will be fine for monitoring those Factors of Success that can help you to accomplish your goal.

Giving rating on your own Factors of Success list is a way to evaluate where you can make improvements, and you can decide to focus with more energy on those Factors of Success that can have the greatest impact on your action plan.

Write down in your logbook your Factors of Success:

- when you are planning your project (Goal Setting).

- when you will act on your tasks (Action).

- when a single task or project is completed (Reviewing).

**Remember**: your Factors of Success are determinants of your plan. Define and choose them in a smart and appropriate way!

# YOUR STRATEGIC RESULT AREAS.

With the Factors of Success, you have learned how to make the difference by choosing the parts that can impact on your actions. Boosting your actions towards your goal *with Strategic Result Areas you can intervene in a specific area that is key to the success in your plan*. The Strategic Result Area can contain one or more Factors of Success.

A Strategic Result Area needs essential knowledge, skills and core competencies connected with one or more areas that help you to succeed.

**Remember:** The Strategic Result Area is an activity that is under your control and you are responsible for it.

**Workout (EXAMPLE)      Date: (EXAMPLE)**

Identify your Strategic Result Areas. Look at this list as an example:

- Equipment, Travel, General or Specific Costs.

- Marketing.

- Public Speaking.

- Video Conferences.

- Books.

- Social Media.

- Experts, Coaches, Mentors.

- Time Management.

**Workout 60**                                         **Date:**

Identify your Strategic Result Areas.

- Having found your Strategic Result Areas, give a grade to each one from 1 to 10. Give 10 to the most important, 9 to the next one, and so on. In this way you can understand which Strategic Result Areas need to be developed.

-Which are your core competencies required for your specific Strategic Result Areas?

-Which is your best developed Strategic Result Area?

-Where are you getting excellent results?

-Where are underperforming?

**Workout 61**                                    **Date:**

Identify your Factors of Success in the most important Strategic Result Area that needs to be developed for your Short and Medium-Term Goals:

# WHAT CAN BLOCK YOU ON THIS STEP?

# THE SEVENTH STEP

## WHEN?

*'I don't think of the misery, but the beauty that still remains.'*

*Anne Frank*

## YOUR TIME AWARENESS.

Having evaluated the appropriate strategy that can impact on your goal with your Action Plan and the Factors of Success, now you need to have a goal deadline, but before establishing an exact date you must understand how you relate to time and how you use it. Our concept of time influences our actions, so it will be necessary to deepen this topic.

How do you consider your time?

How you consider your time is important because it is a precious resource that even if it seems unlimited is never enough. Your awareness of time influences your goals, lifestyle, health and relationships, but above all it is an indicator of the meaning that you give to your life and your ability to pursue a personal vision.

Think what kind of person you are: do you wake up early in the morning or do you go to sleep late at night? Perhaps you have more psychophysical energies during the day, or you feel more vigorous and full of energy in the evening or at night-time.

Your conception of time will not be the same throughout the different ages of your life. When you were a child your time awareness was different from now, then it will change again in future years.

As you know, many people choose a profession that matches their concept of time; unfortunately, it isn't always possible to follow this desire and the consequences are stress, irritability and a sense of tiredness. Little by little these symptoms will influence your lifestyle and your vitality.

Complete the test by answering the questions. The results give you a summary of both your awareness of time and how you use it. Give a rank from 1 to 5.

| totally 5 often 4 enough 3 almost never 2 never 1 |
|---|

| | |
|---|---|
| 1) I am not thinking about the past. | |
| 2) I think my life is pre-destined. | |
| 3) I think life is a challenge. | |
| 4) What happens to me is out of my control. | |
| 5) Everything is repeated in my life without change. | |
| 6) In my life things are never repeated or the same. | |
| 7) I plan my future. | |
| 8) I prepare what I have to do in advance. | |
| 9) I continue to do the same thing. | |

| | |
|---|---|
| 10) I'm sure that everything happens because it is destiny. | |
| 11) I want to be prepared to be ready for future changes. | |
| 12) I do not reflect too much on my past. | |
| 13) I like being on time. | |
| 14) I don't worry about my future. | |
| 15) Everything in my life seems like it just happens. | |
| 16) Striving to improve is useless as nothing changes. | |

## Are you an early riser or a night owl?

| | |
|---|---|
| 17) I prefer activities during the day. | |
| 18) I prefer activities during the afternoon. | |
| 19) I prefer activities during the evening and night. | |
| 20) I am full of energy all day. | |
| 21) I am full of energy in the evening and at night. | |
| 22) I am full of energy in the morning. | |

## Your lifestyle and personal behaviour typology.

| | |
|---|---|
| 23) I complain to others if things do not go as I want. | |
| 24) I learn from my experiences. | |
| 25) I only do the necessary and nothing more. | |
| 26) I like to control the work of others. | |

## How to read your results.

Look at the question numbers and record your score for each one in the boxes. Now add up your total (out of 20) for each line.

- Linear Awareness of Time:

| 7 | | 8 | | 11 | | 13 | | Total___ |
|---|---|---|---|---|---|---|---|---|

- Cyclical type Awareness of Time:

| 3 | | 5 | | 9 | | 15 | | Total___ |
|---|---|---|---|---|---|---|---|---|

- Occasional Awareness of Time:

| 1 | | 6 | | 12 | | 14 | | Total___ |
|---|---|---|---|---|---|---|---|---|

- A closed-type linear time awareness:

| 2 | | 4 | | 10 | | 16 | | Total___ |
|---|---|---|---|----|---|----|---|--------|

The type of time awareness with the highest rating is in line with your profile which is not definitive and may change in the future.

The test results must be seen in the context of your current situation which is influenced by your past and the choices you have made.

Each situation can be improved and changed over time. In fact, the purpose of these workouts is to help you to understand how you can best impose your energy and personal resources in view of your goal; understanding if you are oriented towards one type of time concept rather than another will help you to assess if your beliefs and your decisions are consistent with the purposes you have set yourself.

In general, orientating yourself on a mixed model is the best strategy, as it allows you to be more flexible in the way you use your time, while respecting your natural inclinations and bio-rhythms. In other words, don't get too attached to one way of thinking.

Small habits, if put into practice every day, will create a lifestyle that is closer to your goal.

So can our concept of time influence our choices?

Those who believe that they can't manage or improve their personal development influence themselves negatively by their thoughts, but above all they will organise their time in a different way from a person who believes with conviction that they can manage their own life and personal development.

Our time awareness is conditioned by the events that we meet in life: for instance, a loss of self-esteem or self-control can be caused by how we experience catastrophic events which we cannot influence directly. This can vary from person to person in a similar situation with different feelings. In fact a period of stress can distort our time awareness.

For example, a resilient person manages time and emotions differently from those who feel oppressed by situations - like those students who are afraid to take an exam at school; the duration of the exam will be interminable to them, while for those who feel well prepared the time may flow faster and perhaps pleasantly.

Rammstedt has defined four types of time awareness attributed to different categories of people with different time orientation.

- Occasional orientation to time: life is lived here and now; the person with this notion isn't aware of the future or the past.

- Cyclical awareness of time: in this case, the past is repeated by the same actions that are always unvarying. In fact, the person deals with the past, present and future in the same way without changing anything.

- A closed-type linear time awareness: it is usually fatalism or destiny that drives the lives and choices of people who have a relationship with time like this. People of this type tend to deny the effectiveness of their choices and actions. In fact, they are not ready to establish goals that require efforts in the long term, and in general they are often ineffective and they give up quite easily.

- Open-type linear time awareness: events in this case are a resource for improvement. Indeed, the type of person with this awareness of time has an effective behaviour for dealing with different situations that occur in the course of life, or at least tends to be resilient.

Obviously these parameters are generic because it is common to find people with a mixed-type time concept. Moreover, as I previously mentioned, the concept of time changes in the course of our life and we have the power to change it.

*What you need for your goal is to clarify how you use your time; the more you have a greater awareness of it the more your influence will affect it and not the other way around. In addition, I would say that the way you use your time indicates the type of life and goals that you set and the kind of person you are.*

The following table will give you a rough indication of your time conception and how you use it.

| Occasional type. | The open linear type. |
|---|---|
| Living with self-efficacy | Being realised |
| Living to achieve goal in life | Being active |
| Being here and now | Having time to do something |
| Being free | Creating something |
| and independent | Making a career |
| Being creative | |
| **The cyclic type.** | **The closed linear type.** |
| Being recognised as a person | Being admired for your efforts |
| Being reliable | Helping others |
| Doing your duty | Doing a job perfectly |
| Feeling part of a group | Being an influential person. |

In principle, people with a profile in the open types of time awareness have more effective behaviour, also reflected in personal fulfilment. Efforts are viewed in an operational context useful for improvement and success. People with this awareness of time are able to assess the causes of their successes or failures, gaining experience and becoming wise.

In the other profiles there is a tendency towards non-change following a pessimistic lifestyle, with results almost nil or that do not lead to any effective improvement in their destiny. These people tend to blame circumstances and other people, and without being responsible for the causes of their problems they risk recreating the same situations created in the past.

In the occasional type of awareness, it is the different opportunities to give impulse to these people with the disadvantage of not giving continuity to their intentions. Moreover, these people are waiting for the right opportunity to do things, but as sometimes happens in life the opportunities escape them and they can't improve their own destiny.

The positive thing for this group of people is that they can have a propensity to creativity and self-fulfilment that can appear at any moment of their lives so that they can be motivated to reach their goals.

The 'Are you an early riser or a night owl?' test helped you understand how you use your energy during the twenty-four hour cycle. Also, it helps us to change a situation while being careful not to break the psychophysical balance of our health. Evaluate if you need to change your habits and ask for advice from an expert.

With the 'Your lifestyle and personal behaviour typology test' you can easily evaluate how you direct your life, based on your beliefs and choices. The test gives four statements that, although not exhaustive if compared to other more complete tests, give you an indication of whether your style of thinking is in line with one of the four profiles.

I want to give you an example: suppose you are one of the people with the occasional concept of time and you have a predisposition to be more active during the night, what kind of activity could you choose to do? Depending on the type of your character you might choose jobs where responsibility is required, or you do only what is needed. What do these two characteristics suggest to you? Could you be a chef or a waiter working in a restaurant until late at night, for instance?

---

**Workout 64**                                    **Date:**

Now, based on the results obtained in the different tests, make your personal profile and assess how you could improve it writing the solutions you would like to apply. At the same time, estimate how your goal can be matched with your personal profile discovered in the tests.

---

## DECIDE YOUR GOAL DEADLINE.

Now that you have understood how you relate to the concept of time and how you use it, it's time to decide a deadline for your goal. In fact, a goal has to have its deadline and the deadline is the only way to create a connection between your idea and the real world where you will act.

*A goal without a timeline isn't a goal but only an idea without consequences for your life.*

---

**Workout 65**                              **Date:**

### WRITE DOWN YOUR DEADLINE!

**My GOAL is:**

**Its DEADLINE is:**        **Signature:**

(You could ask another person to sign your goal deadline so you have a 'witness' who can support you and give you his or her feedback.)

I suggest you make a poster with your deadline.

---

## Break down your GOAL into STEPS!

Often our goals can be complex so we need to break them down into steps; by following this strategy we can stay focused and work little by little, one step at time, until it is completed and reviewed. Working in steps is a good way of monitoring your progress and taking control of your actions; in addition, you can work on your project without being scared of its complexity.

You need to lay out your goal in steps through different periods of time. Knowing what you want to achieve periodically is very important because you can stay on your pathway, accomplishing your *sub-goals* every week or every month. In this way you can find the motivation that you need.

With the explanation above I now want to introduce you to the concept of short, medium and long-term goals.

*SHORT-TERM GOAL:* when you are in the presence of a short-term goal it doesn't require a big effort to achieve it in its allotted period of time. Though when you start with the first step, it is possible that you will feel exhausted, under pressure, insecure or confused about what to do.

**Remember:** *the first step is the most important on your road of success!*

Without it it is impossible to get going and go ahead, so be brave and take action. A short-term goal could be to study ten pages every day for one month so you can pass your geography exam.

*MEDIUM-TERM GOAL:* following the example above, the geography exam is probably not the only one that you have to take. In reality it is a part of your education programme and you have to study more subjects during the year and take more exams. Your geography exam is part of a medium-term goal which is made up of multiple steps in short-term goals. Usually a medium-term goal is a period of three months, so every three months you can complete your medium-term goals. During a year you can create four medium-term goals that contains a certain number of short-term goals.

*LONG-TERM GOAL:* we can define a long-term goal as a period of at least one year. You can decide to set your long-term goal for a longer period, like two years, five years, ten years or more.

A long-term goal can cover all areas of your life like your competencies, your relationships and your autonomy. In this case it will be useful to develop your spiritual strengths that will allow you to raise the inner power and the energy you will need to accomplish your goal.

*A long-term goal requires great determination and sacrifices that won't guarantee success, but with your persistence and determination you can make the difference until it is achieved.*

Your long-term goal is represented by the entire length of your road of success. It always starts from your VISION.

**Remember:** when you accomplish a goal, you have completed a Term Goal Cycle that can restart with a new goal, a new vision and a new mission. Your goals need to be very detailed and you can have one or more Factors of Success. You can work out your steps in an appropriate way for you creating your own model, creating your sub-goals within each type of goal: short, medium or long term.

**Workout 66**                                  **Date:**

## YOUR ROAD MAP TO SUCCESS.

Your LONG-TERM GOAL is your vision:

Your MEDIUM-TERM GOALS: create your sub-goals and decide what can help you to make the difference.

## Your SHORT-TERM GOALS.

These are the goals that you need to start now! Start from your short-term goals and proceed towards your long-term goal. Be ready to create the best sub-goals.

# WHAT CAN BLOCK YOU ON THIS STEP?

Your options and solutions:

# THE EIGHTH STEP.

## WHERE?

*'It doesn't matter where you are coming from. All that matters is where you are going.'*

*Brian Tracy*

## WHERE DO YOU WANT TO ACHIEVE YOUR GOAL?

The following questions are useful because you can understand and monitor where you want to create your project and where you are at this moment on your road to success. The first question is about the place where you intend to spend your time, putting your plan into action and achieving your goal. The place where you will realise your project is important so you need to choose the right place for you. For instance, a town with an excellent university or an area with many start-ups that can match your need to improve your professional development and reach your ambitions.

| Workout 67 | Date: |
| --- | --- |

WHERE DO YOU WANT TO ACHIEVE YOUR GOAL?

Now, think about your current environment and make a list of what it can offer to you (or what you can do to improve the place where you are living) in accordance to your goal. Write down the positive and negative aspects of the place where you live and now do the same thing for the future place that you think is right to you.

**Workout 68**                                      **Date:**

Use this example to describe both your current place and the place where you intend to go in the future.

The place where I am now.

| Positive aspects. | Negative aspects. |
|---|---|
|  |  |

The place where I wish to be in the future.

| Positive aspects. | Negative aspects. |
| --- | --- |
|  |  |

The second question aims to help you to evaluate if you know where you are on your project at the moment by monitoring your progress.

---

**Workout 69**                                    **Date:**

WHERE ARE YOU ON THE ROAD TO SUCCESS?

---

# WHAT CAN BLOCK YOU ON THIS STEP?

## THE NINTH STEP.

### THE POWER OF ACTION!

*'However difficult life may seem, there is always something you can do and succeed at.'*

*Stephen Hawking*

## I WISH, I DREAM, I WANT, I REACH IT!

*'Pay attention to the words you use every day, especially when you think about the desires that you want to make happen. As you think, you act.'*

It is right to desire as well as to dream and want something, but it is not enough to give you the great power to achieve what you are aiming for. What can give you this great power then? Your mind!

Pay attention to the words you use in formulating your desire, your vision and goals.

If you only think of dreaming your mind will lead you just to dream and you won't act to make your dream happen in reality. In fact, if you just wish for something your mind will continue to guide you to many other desires without goals which may be broadly related but are not exactly what you want, and this can confuse your brain. If you really want to take action you have to give a specific command to your mind. So, you can realise your goal with this great power:

*your mind needs a stimulus to act!*

What do you do at this point to turn on the mind and give an impulse to the body to act? Try to say: '*I'm doing it!*'

**Remember:** give your command like this in the present tense. As human beings we are destined for action and just saying 'I want it' doesn't work for our mind which loves to bring us to new goals through action. By saying 'I'm doing it!' you will feel more motivated to act and it is action you need to achieve your goals, isn't it?

| SUCCESS REQUIRES: |
| :---: |
| Self-Awareness |
| Self-Discipline |
| Self-Control |
| Self-Mastery |

You have to evaluate how your character, thoughts, emotions, feelings, beliefs, strengths, weaknesses and behaviour can impact on your goal. This kind of mindset is called *self-awareness.* Self-awareness plays an important role when you make changes in your life, and if you want to succeed it is very important to understand yourself better; in fact, self-awareness allows you to see how you lead your life. In achieving your goal you need to develop your self-awareness and your self-control. Both self-awareness and self-control are connected: the more aware you are about yourself, the more you have the power to take control of your own feelings, desires and behaviours, with many advantages in any situation. How can you develop or improve your self-control being aware of your emotions, temptations and impulses?

*'Self-control is strength. Right thought is mastery. Calmness is power.'*

James Allen

**Remember:** *self-control* can be developed with practice and training, having a lot of benefits such as:

- reducing your reactions and impulsive behaviours.
- improving your mental focus and your decision making ability.
- renewing your mindset.
- taking your emotions and feelings under control.
- improving your relationships.

Understanding the importance of taking control of your life is really important, but it isn't enough if you want to empower yourself. You need to increase your *self-discipline* level.

First of all, learn how to take the right actions in accordance with your personal promises to yourself and your commitment to your goal. Motivate yourself to follow your standards, vision and mission about your goal; train yourself step by step to do the things you know you should do, even when you hate those things. Following this rule you will see determination and persistence increase.

I have known a lot of people with a high level of knowledge, skills, preparation, attitude and motivation who were ready to achieve something in their lives, but some of them have given up on their dreams. Why?

They had a lack of self-discipline. Nothing else determines your success in life quite as much as the ability to be self-disciplined.

Self-discipline is a mental strength: when you are self-disciplined, it indicates that your thoughts, emotions, feelings, reactions, behaviours and desires are under control, but this is only possible if you are able to motivate yourself to face situations, relationships and problems that need to be addressed. This willpower can help you to persevere in your projects and personal development, overcoming difficulties and obstacles. Self-discipline is very helpful especially when you want to accomplish long-term goals - then it will be possible to do boring tasks that need to be completed urgently. This situation could be painful: I remember the fatigue of writing many hours per week under tiredness and with lack of sleep. How did I manage this?

I understood that all my efforts and expectations would be rewarded once I achieved my dream of finishing my first book in English about personal development. I didn't always feel comfortable or self-disciplined but it was the only way to achieve my goal. I learned how to manage against fatigue, laziness and excuses that could stop me - such as avoiding boring tasks that were necessary for my dream.

I can say that this experience has improved me as person. In fact, I know how to resist temptations and to take my reactions under control in different situations.

Temptations, lack of purpose or low self-confidence are the main enemies when you need to stay on the road to success: *if you don't have enough willpower to change your bad habits it will be difficult to realise your goal.* So be prepared to train yourself to develop the skill of self-discipline, leading yourself in continuous improvement with small steps that can allow you to become mentally strong!

Successful people become mentally stronger because they are able to discipline themselves to work consistently towards their goals.

*Transform self-discipline into a habit and you will attract success in your life, boosting your strengths, self-esteem and confidence.*

**Workout 70**                                    **Date:**

How can you become more disciplined and mentally strong? Think about these points and how to apply them to yourself.

- Be aware about yourself: stay focused and develop your self-awareness level.

- Train yourself step by step in small tasks with different difficulty levels.

- Monitor the level achieved and restart with other tasks where the difficulty is greater.

- Learn how to avoid temptation: use meditation and mindfulness.

- Reward yourself after achieving your goals in proportion to the effort used to complete all the tasks.

- Train yourself to remove all distractions that can delay your tasks, and monitor your bad habits which can damage your self-improvement or your project.

**Self-Mastery: how to become the master of your destiny.**

Self-mastery is a process and it develops after long experience. It requires humility, self-awareness, self-control and self-discipline. Becoming your own master you will feel more confident, mature and open minded - a person who knows the road to take.

*'...You can't become successful with the personality you currently have. Allow yourself to learn who you really are by paying attention to the voice and force within you. Then you can become what you are fated to become. An individual - A master.'*

*Robert Greene.*

Living an ordinary life without any change or just accepting all the situations around us is a choice that doesn't make any contributions to our lives. A lot of people don't accomplish any goals in their lives, but as Greene explains we have the power to become the master of our destiny if we understand the importance of making efforts to improve ourselves. Self-mastery can elevate our status and power as individuals. Your inner power can always emerge if you are ready to follow your passion; you will discover another version of yourself, such as becoming more confident with a lot of energy and enthusiasm.

Always ask yourself if the knowledge you have can satisfy the standards required by your vision and your goal: with *The 10 Amazing Steps to Success* you have the tools that can allow you to stay focused on what you are doing or learning now. Surround yourself with positive people who have experience, to teach you how to learn the best way to achieve the lifestyle, knowledge and skills that you need.

# THE SECRET TO ALWAYS BEING MOTIVATED.

*Being motivated and enthusiastic is the way to take action.*

I remember when I wrote this book that I slept only a few hours each day and I was very busy with my work as a cleaner and caretaker at my school, but it didn't disturb me or my life balance because I was so determined to complete the book.

A mix of enthusiasm and persistence were the powers that allowed me to write my book, because it was something wonderful that I had never imagined doing in my life.

I challenged myself because I wanted to be a strong role model for the Ark Academy's kids during my time as a volunteer performance coach.

If you are enthusiastic about your goal you won't feel tired: your mind will drive you to find the right balance and the appropriate solutions in managing your new challenge.

**Remember:** your enthusiasm drives you into action and it will help you to transform your fatigue into enjoyment of your work.

I want to suggest you use visualisation: visualising your actions before you take action is a good way to prepare your brain and your body to be ready when you start on your tasks.

**Workout 71** Date:

Imagine yourself during your tasks, starting from the first one until the last one is completed. Make a note of any details or important ideas that you have imagined during your visualisation.

The aim is to prevent any reactions such as wavering commitment or delaying things unnecessarily that can become frustrating or can damage your tasks. You will manage your feelings better during your actions because you have prepared yourself beforehand with this workout.

## How can you always be being motivated?

- With Selection: select your Factors of Success and be selective with your tasks; consider which of them requires your attention and think about their impact on your plan.

- With Persistence: keep a high level of personal commitment based on your strengths and vision. Be happy to do the things that you are doing and remember that your own satisfaction is more important than your goal.

 - With Intensity: high motivation drives you to an excellent work rate to deliver success. Don't consider intensity as something that you have to do with a huge amount of effort sacrificing your own life balance. The intensity that you need refers to your feelings and emotions during your favourite tasks.

-With Flow: being in the 'state of mind' and fully immersed during your performance of the task.

- With Balance: control your need to achieve and the fear of failure.

It may happen that it is not always possible to stay motivated all the time so don't lose your concentration. Giving your personal rating to your motivators, you will be able to develop those motivators that are necessary to your improvement and motivation.

---

**Workout 72**                                    **Date:**

Rate yourself for each word in this list from 1 to 10.

Selection:

Persistence:

Intensity:

Flow:

Balance:

---

**Workout 73**                                              **Date:**

Describe in a few sentences what can help you to stay motivated during your project towards your goal. Then make your own list of your most important motivators.

## BE PROACTIVE: TAKE ACTION!

*Be proactive: do the things you hate. Act on the things you can influence rather than reacting to external forces.*

Do not focus only on your favourite tasks but complete all the tasks that can allow you to achieve your goal as Brian Tracy has recommended in his books. Indeed, you need to follow the order of your tasks, not avoiding or leaving the tasks that you think aren't important just because you feel they aren't enjoyable or exciting.

Consider breaking down your current task and allowing yourself to have a reward when it is completed, and try to link your task with nice emotions, learning from each step how to feel satisfied.

*Your Success is close if you are able to move all your FACTORS of SUCCESS into EXCELLENCE!*

**Workout 74**                                    **Date:**

Today I need to do these tasks because they are important parts of my goal... although I hate them:

# THE POMODORO TECHNIQUE.

The Pomodoro Technique is perfect for you because you can monitor your efforts and your personal commitment to stay focused on the daily tasks in your project. Now, I wish to show you how this method works: The Pomodoro Technique is a method that is used in time management and it was invented by the Italian Francesco Cirillo in 1980. It is a gorgeous tool that uses a kitchen timer to make a break during tasks or jobs, with intervals every twenty-five minutes. It is very useful especially when you have to stay focused for a long period of time, or when you need to strategically overcome your procrastination. Using this method you can work for a certain length of time on your tasks, and having to respect your timeline every twenty-five or forty-five minutes you don't have any reason to be interrupted.

**Workout 75** Date:

- Decide your daily tasks to be completed and set the timer of your clock, app or kitchen timer for twenty-five or forty-five minutes.

- Start work on one task with maximum effort and focus.

- When the timer rings it is time to have a break, but it mustn't be more than five minutes!

-Reset your timer so it can restart to count another twenty-five or forty-five minutes.

-Repeat this operation in accordance with the length of your task.

-Make a record of how many times you have interrupted your task.

## THE PARETO PRINCIPLE.

Vilfredo Paredo, an Italian economist, published this idea for the first time. It was rediscovered by the management consultant Joseph M. Juran, but with Richard Koch we have the modern use of this principle as we know it as nowadays it is used in business and life management.

Successful people use 20% of their time to reach 80% of their goals! Indeed, people who use 80% of their time in the wrong way will achieve only 20% of their goals!

---

**Workout 76**                                    **Date:**

Ask yourself: are you spending a lot of time on less important activities in the lower 80% of priority, or are you spending enough time on the most urgent work in the top 20%? Record your own activities.

For example: I spent two hours on advertising... (20% of my time). I spent eight hours on reading social media posts... (80% of my time). This means that I spent my time on unimportant things? Yes!

---

Today the 20% of my time was spent on...




Am I doing the most important things regularly?

Today the 80% of my time was spent on...

I discovered something more about the Pareto Principle: *you have to choose what is really necessary for your goal, being focused on the most important tasks at the time.*

It means that you need to select where to focus if you want to accomplish your goal faster, managing your time in an excellent way. In fact, doing the tasks that can really impact on your life or project gives you the opportunity to achieve more. Choose the most important task that represents the top 20% because it will allow you to gain the 80% of your goal!

This principle works only if you are able to select the right steps and making all the efforts required in an effective way. The Pareto Principle can help you to simplify your project with less effort and more results.

Learn to simplify. Learning how to simplify helps your efficacy.

If you want to be efficient you need to simplify your thoughts, your actions and your tasks. Considering what is necessary for your proposal is the best option because it isn't necessary to do everything that you have thought or planned. So cancel what is superfluous!

Ask yourself if other options, solutions or strategies can help you to overcome any delays in your project.

So as not to be focused just on the details, maybe you could co-operate with experts who can complete certain parts of your project or you can evaluate which tasks need to be eliminated because they aren't linked appropriately with your goal.

## C.A.R.S. Critical Analysis of Risks and Success. ©

*Do not be perfect, be effective.*

The critical analysis of risks and success is like making a survey analysis along the entire path made up to the current moment.

On the one hand foreseeing the risks helps you to prevent, avoid, circumnavigate or solve them. On the other hand, it is important to analyse your success connected with the various steps of your goal during the short, medium and long-term goals.

How can you benefit from the C.A.R.S. method?

Applying the C.A.R.S. method gives you enormous advantages in your life and projects.

- You will be being focused on what is necessary to achieve your goal.

- You save your energy, effort and time.

- You have a clear pathway towards every step of your action plan.

- You can create a practical method that allows you to monitor your actions and tasks at any time during your project.

- You will be prepared to use your Factors of Success in a brilliant way.

- You will be able to avoid or circumnavigate the risks that can delay your project.

The C.A.R.S. Method gives you the personal power that you need if you want to succeed.

Motivation has a profound power over us and with it we can realise anything, but without adequate preparation every good intention can clash with harsh reality. Through the many adversities that we encounter in life, sooner or later our resistance, concentration and motivation will be put to the test. How can you keep your motivation high? How do you know your progress? How can you be sure to take the road to success?

If you want to succeed you have to monitor your progress and performance in a way that allows you to increase your motivation level and take control of the strategic areas of your project step by step through your factors of success.

The C.A.R.S. Method is an easy approach that allows to you to take control over your actions and all the detailed parts of your project:

- make an orderly sequence for your tasks.

- monitor the tasks done and the impact they make on your action plan, learning how to do better in the next task.

Let's see how The C.A.R.S. Method works.

The C.A.R.S. Method follows these important strategic steps: outline, preparation, action and monitor.

## Outline:

- Outline all your Factors of Success such as your own strengths, your skills and your equipment.

- Pay attention to your weak areas.

- Measure your performances and grade yourself in all areas that are represented by your Factors of Success so you can be ready to improve at any time.

## Preparation:

- It means that you can intervene in your weak areas but you have to be clear in mind what your current standard or level is. This can allow to you to improve your performance in those areas you need to be successful.

In this phase you can evaluate your personal scores for your preparation.

- Evaluate your current performance standard level.

- Set an action plan to allow you to improve them in a well-defined period of time.

- Check your equipment properly!

### Action:

The only way is to act immediately. Taking action every day is the basis for progress towards your goal. Focus on the actions that can impact positively on your goal, following all your criteria set out in your action plan.

### Monitor:

It is important not to monitor your performance or your sub-goals too early. If the period between your performance and your measurement is too short it is impossible to have enough data for an objective overview.

*Your performances need to be developed according to your next level and your expectations.* If you don't consider this aspect properly you can lose your motivation or determination because you won't see any improvement. So it is much better to prepare a time schedule for your measurements such as at the end of every each month, recording your performance and the tasks done in your logbook. Monitoring all your factors of success gives you an overview of those areas that haven't made any progress. You can then consider if you need to improve all areas to work on or to choose only the ones that can really boost your performance and goal.

Once this process is finished and all its parts are completed you can start again with new tasks following the same order having a series of actions that will lead you towards the realisation of your goal in a more efficient way.

| Your Personal Power of Success Method. |
|---|

**Workout 77**                                    **Date:**

| 1-Outline: | 2-Preparation: |
|---|---|
| 4-Monitor: | 3-Action: |

Use the table to record the main steps. I advise you to dedicate the necessary time to describing the various steps once you have completed them. You can repeat this workout in future whenever you want to monitor new projects or other sub-goals in the same project.

Imagine having the power to see so far that you could see the whole of your life from beginning to end. What would you see? Surely you would see all the situations and events and all the actions that you have done in succession.

To date there is no way to see your life as I have just mentioned, but fortunately there are techniques supported by tests that allow us to create models with which it is possible to predict some aspects of a project.

The C.A.R.S. Method that I have created can help you to monitor the critical points of your action plan better with countless benefits.

It is based on: *the critical path method (CPM) or critical path analysis (CPA), an algorithm for scheduling a set of project activities. It is commonly used in conjunction with the programme evaluation and review technique.*

This C.P.M. technique was developed by Morgan R. Walker DuPont and James E. Kelley in the 1950s. The Critical Path Analysis is used with different kinds of projects like construction, aerospace, software development, research projects, product development, engineering and plant maintenance among others. Any project with interdependent activities can apply this method with analytical software.

How can you use this technique in your life and in your project even if you do not have the C.P.M. software that allows you to manage all the data related to your case?

I will give you an example of this system and how it could be applied.

Imagine a hypothetical situation in emergency care in a hospital casualty department. In some instances the lack of certain equipment or personnel could lead to a patient's death in the worst case scenario. Therefore, there are protocols for treatment - things to be checked and actions to be taken. These form a critical pathway including every detail that could make the difference between life and death.

It is backed up by constant checks on the equipment and simple things such as updating the phone numbers of those who can replace medical staff in case of unexpected absence. Then every need for people and materials has been provided, and the steps for monitoring and treatment are clearly laid out and followed - leading to the best possible outcomes.

Of course in your own life the process will not be as complicated as running a hospital but the same principles apply.


Now you can use this system for your project too!

The specific characteristics of this model are mainly to monitor and prevent possible errors or delays, but also to choose the strategy that you consider most effective to reduce the execution time of your project.

Let's see in detail how it works: *The C.P.M. is used to construct a model of the basic project that determines which activities are 'critical', a process at considers every step in the project's pathway.* In project management a critical path is:

- the sequence of project activities which add up to the longest overall duration.

- the critical path can then determine the shortest possible time to complete the project.

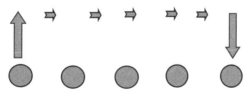

Any delay to an activity on the critical path directly impacts on the planned completion date.

Based on this system, The C.A.R.S. Method allows you to construct a model of your project that includes:

- *A list of all the activities* required to complete the project. (In addition you can use the Eisenhower Model, paying attention to the tasks that it will be possible to do urgently, postpone, delegate or eliminate, and using the S.W.O.T. analysis you can monitor any risks on your pathway.)

- *The time (duration) that each activity will take to complete.* One activity can have a different execution time from another.

- *The connections between the activities.* Ask yourself which activities could be carried out together or which have an ordered series of connections which can have consequences for each other.

Using this information you can calculate:

- The longest path of your activities until the end of the project. For instance, if you need more time to complete one task than others it could affect the duration of all your activities.

*You can decide which strategy can help you at any moment and change one or more steps of your action plan on the basis of your needs without making the project longer!*

In fact having analysed where you are now on your project, and knowing your deadline and the various steps that you need to complete, you have a clear idea about the execution time of your entire project (or single parts of it such as the sub-goals in short-medium-long-term goals), respecting the final date to complete it.

With the C.A.R.S. Method you can make an accurate analysis of Critical Points that give you the right overview of:

- those strategies that are or aren't in accordance with your project.

- any delays that can stop you.

- the threats that you could meet during your project and in every step of it.

- the pathways that are unproductive and those you can cancel.

- the entire project if it doesn't respect your ideas.

- if your actions follow your project and if they are effective.

**Remember:** all details are important. Focus on the ones that allow you to achieve your goal better and faster, paying attention to timing and to your efforts to complete your entire project.

> How I applied The C.A.R.S. Method
> and the tools on this book.

When I decided to write my book I was so enthusiastic that I wanted to do everything, write the book, create its cover, talk in public about my book (that wasn't written yet), editing, publishing the book on kindle and learning how to sell it!

It was impossible to do everything and if I had tried, certainly today, my dear friend, you would not have the opportunity to read this book as I would have lost my drive and enthusiasm.

I realised what I had to stay focused on. I decided that my most important task was just to write the book... within a month. Yes, I wrote my book in just a month!

I understood that I had to put all my energies and efforts on the first factor of success about my project: the most important task was writing the book. Obviously, along the way I created other factors of success. What had I put into practice?

Fortunately, I applied criteria and steps that I had studied in personal development and in life coaching. In fact, I decided to analyse what could interest my readers, and the most important thing was the right strategies that they could apply in achieving their goals. I wanted to write interesting chapters without boring descriptions but enriched with people's stories and with numerous workouts, so I began *to select* all the information I needed.

Then I had to finish my tasks within a certain *time,* and I used the Eisenhower Method to eliminate all unnecessary things that could delay my project... like reading many emails every day!

I decided to write my book during my spare time and at night. I promised myself to focus only on writing the book for at least three hours a day. But, dear friend, believe me, to write for a few hours a day doesn't seem too much, but after a month fatigue and lack of sleep are felt. So I had to take care of myself.

As the training theory explains, after writing every single chapter I planned to have some spare time and relax, and this strategy was decisive for my result. In fact, I wrote the book with less effort and fatigue.

I applied Pareto's Method with the maximum result: I removed the superfluous where it was necessary and I focused on 20% of my time and actions that could impact positively on my goal. This strategy was possible because I used the Pomodoro technique too. I set my alarm clock for thirty minute intervals so that I could be focused for a short period of time giving my best. Obviously, every thirty minutes I took a break of at least five minutes so I was energised to restart on my task.

The month was passing quickly and in the meantime my mind was back to thinking about editing and the marketing plan, but I couldn't allow my mind to take control of the situation.

Recourse *to monitor the threats on the project* about my book. The risk was related to my inability to do everything; if I decided to spend time editing the book for instance, I would have lost my concentration and energy for no result.

At the same time I saved my draft numerous times and I used multiple devices as well as a paper version so as not to take the risk of losing the work already done, or I backed the file up on a USB memory stick.

Little by little I realised that I was on the right track. In fact, the goal of publishing my book within a few months became realistic!

Furthermore, I did not review my book until I had finished writing it, and I delegated the task of re-checking the English to my English tutor.

I created a winning model that could allow me to follow all my criteria and steps without a waste of time and energy. In fact, with The C.A.R.S. Method, I could monitor all my performances in the end of each goal term. I continually optimised what I was doing, improving or simplifying my book, and I was able to control the whole process directly, understanding which actions could delay my project or boost it.

I would like to invite you to apply the C.A.R.S. Method and the tools explained in this chapter so you can analyse what can stop or delay your steps. Remember, before starting on your task you have to consider the entire length of time that will be necessary to complete it. For example, five weeks.

E.g. 5 weeks.

The numbered blocks represent the various steps to your final goal.

As you know, sometimes it is possible to choose to overcome or circumnavigate barriers or limitations, especially if you meet circumstances that can delay your project, or you can decide to eliminate what

419

isn't necessary to your project. Maybe you are able to do the same things in only four weeks, for example, just because you eliminated what isn't important to your project.

At the same time it is useful to analyse your Technical Equipment and evaluate your goal's priorities with the Four Ps. Learn how to organise your tasks with the Eisenhower Method so you can have an appropriate process in which it is easy be focused during your activities.

Your decision to finish your project in just a few weeks will only be possible if your preparation allows you to proceed. Do things in the right order with the purpose of monitoring your tasks so you can check what works.

**Remember:** *you may find that with just one factor of success you can achieve more without a complicated action plan, delegating other tasks to experts.*

Using the C.A.R.S. Method is a winning strategy. You can evaluate what can make the difference in your project. It is a good habit to record any improvement and success as much as what went wrong during your action plan.

Having accumulated experience, you can plan your future project carefully with a clear road map regarding what can work or not work for your next goal.

Think and draw your project map with the C.A.R.S. Method, considering the critical points such as:

- the start and end date of the project.

- the steps that you need to take.

- the critical activities that are vital to your project.

- the duration that each activity will take to complete.

- the interdependencies between the activities.

- the short and long critical pathways in your project which can give different results.

- any delays that can make your project longer.

- the threats and barriers that could delay your project or part of it.

- options that can help you to overcome any delay and barriers during your project.

**Monitor the threats on your project.**

Sometimes it is not possible to foresee all the risks that may appear during your project. Usually these risks are noticed only after finishing our tasks with possible repercussions on the entire project, or with delays in the phases of execution. One solution is to predict threats to your preparation and performance during the planning.

Monitoring the threats that can arise during your performance is an excellent way to prevent any problems, delays and barriers in your project. The idea is to have a clear overview of the risks occurring during the timeframe of your goals, making a list that considers all kinds of threats along with their solutions.

For example:

| Threat to performance. | Solution to the threat. |
|---|---|
| If my motorbike battery runs down. | Then I will use battery cables to recharge it. |
| If a front lamp gets broken. | Then I will use another new lamp. |
| If I lose my gloves. | Then I will have another pair with me. |

**Workout 79**                                    **Date:**

Now try it for your project:

| Threat to performance. | Solution to the threat. |
|---|---|
|  |  |

# WHAT CAN BLOCK YOU ON THIS STEP?

- The fear of success that can create self-sabotage.

- The fear of failure.

- The beliefs that can damage your motivation.

### So, identify what can block you.

- Not doing what I need to reach my goal.

- Not having enough self-awareness.

- Not having self-discipline, self-control, self-mastery.

- Not describing and not prescribing.

- Not acting and monitoring your goal.

- Not being motivated.

- Not being proactive Continuing to procrastinate.

- Not using your time properly and efficiently.

## THE TENTH STEP:

THE ACHIEVER:

_____

MY FINAL GOAL
HAS BEEN REACHED!

IT IS TIME TO CELEBRATE!

Date:

## GIVE A PRIZE
## FOR YOUR ACHIEVED GOALS!

Being successful at every term goal (whether short, medium or long term) is important because it can allow you to maintain a high level of motivation, commitment and persistence. Celebrate your victory with a prize that must be commensurate with the goal achieved and the effort made. The prizes are milestones along your road of success.

**Workout 80**                                    **Date:**

**Celebrate your short, medium and long-term goals.**

| |
|---|
| My prize for my first goal achieved in the short-term goals: |
| My prize for my first goal achieved in the medium-term goals: |
| My prize for my big goal achieved at the end of my project: |
| The people I want to be thankful to are: |
| My Big Celebration will be on... |

> **The ability to replicate success.**

The mark of excellence is not the ability to deliver a one-off success, it is the ability to replicate success.

This will be possible if you have created your personal achievement model. It allows you to examine the factors that can limit or block you. At the same time, it gives you an overview of your Strategic Areas and where to focus. By following the steps in their right order, you can take control of the details.

**Remember:** every step is of equal importance and you can use this model any time to start new projects.

Always follow these steps:

## THE TOWER OF SUCCESS

| |
|---|
| YOUR VISION |
| YOUR MOTIVATION |
| YOUR FACTORS OF SUCCESS |
| YOUR BEST ACTION PLAN |
| YOUR PREPARATION |
| YOUR ACTION |
| YOUR MONITORING |
| YOUR CELEBRATING & REVIEWING! |

## REVIEW YOUR GOALS.

In each steps of your goal you need to monitor your:

- success

- unsuccess

- risks

 and find options or solutions so your C.A.R.S. Method will be very powerful!

Write down in your logbook the aspects of your challenge that were successful and unsuccessful so you can have an overview of them.

This workout (number 80) gives you excellent information for your current and future projects.

Record the goal step: describing if it was successful or unsuccessful, the risks you met, the options and the solutions you have taken. Then, try to think alternative solution for future plan.

| Step or Goal | Success | Non success | Risks | Option | Solution | Solution for future plan |
|---|---|---|---|---|---|---|
|  |  |  |  |  |  |  |

## REFLECT ON YOUR SUCCESS.

Reflecting on your achieved goals is the best way to have an overview of your entire project, your efforts, your strategies and the failures you have managed. It will allow you to find new options that you didn't think of during your project, options that will make the difference in future experiences.

**Workout 81**                                    **Date:**

My reflection on my success:

434

# THE BENEFITS AND THE ADVANTAGES I GOT FROM MY GOAL.

Workout 82                                        Date:

Dear friend, I am really excited to say that I am happy to have helped you to reach your goals, thus achieving things that make your dreams come true. If you have not achieved anything in these months, I invite you to persevere and to evaluate positively your experience to date. I am grateful to you, dear friend, for having dedicated your time to yourself and for having used my book during your personal and human growth. I hope you can be happy and be inspired by other people in the future!

### REMEMBER:

During your journey along your road to success you have learned how to embrace failure; failing is how you learn. Note carefully the importance of changing the way you think about failures, because your failures are steps on your pathway to reach success; your mistakes aren't negatives if you have the courage to learn from them.

My mother Teresa Feo taught me:

'cadi, ti fai male e ti rialzi.'

In English it sounds like 'you fall, you get hurt and you get up'!

*Replace 'failure' with 'temporary defeat'.*

*'Take care of yourself, you will spend energies and you will make efforts to achieve your goal at the risk of sacrificing your time without the people you love.*

*'But if you have the ability to find your balance during your challenge, having positive enjoyable moments with yourself and the people you love, you will have fantastic memories for your entire life!'*

**Never give up
and BE GRATEFUL!**
*Cristian Cairo*

*'Choose to live in Joy'.*

*Life goes by in the blink of an eye.*

*It's too short to live upset, angry, resentful or ungrateful. If you look for the good, you'll find it. Choose to be happy, to be at peace.*

*Decide that each day is going to be a great day and grab each moment and make the best of it. Refuse to let negative thoughts take root in your mind and refuse to let negative people and situations drag you down. Trust your journey and know that if you make a mistake, it is OK. See it as a lesson learned and keep moving forward. Spend less time worrying and more time being grateful for those who love you and all of life's goodness. Choose to live in joy!*

*Charity M. Richey-Bentley*

**EXTRA CONTENTS.**

Do you know what the reasons for your procrastination are?

E.g. Tiredness, overloading yourself, false beliefs, confusion, not being confident, losing your motivation...

**Workout 83**                            **Date:**

    Try to explain why you are procrastinating.

As Dr. Fuschia Sirois, a researcher at the University of Sheffield in the psychology of health, has shown, putting off some of your tasks from time to time is a normal behaviour but this can become a real problem when you start to procrastinate all the time and you don't complete your work.

She has explained that you can assess when it is time to be worried about your procrastination that can damage your health and your aims in life.

How can you identify if you're really procrastinating?

Real procrastination is when you decide to avoid something that is important and necessary to you and you 'deliberately' avoid it not caring about the consequences.

This problem happens especially when you 'decide' to avoid some activities that can be related to negative emotions and feelings such as the fear of success or the fear of failure; you can consider whether your procrastination has a subconscious origin.

You need to be aware when you prefer to do something that isn't really important and of little reward. For instance, when using social media or watching TV for many hours a day instead of focusing on your real priorities.

We may do this with a false belief that it is 'just once'. But if you continue to repeat this kind of behaviour you will risk ruining your personal self-esteem. In fact, if you believe that it is 'just once' and you don't get your priority job done, in future it will be impossible to complete your journey on the road to success, but you may find only the road to failure.

Another kind of procrastination is to continue to engage in daydreaming instead of being active and working on your proposal. Be aware because your brain can believe that your imaginings are real. So what can happen?

*Your brain convinces itself that you just have accomplished your dream, your desire or your goal. But it is unreal!*

In its own way this can cause your procrastination because it is very hard to start something that your brain believes is already done.

**Remember:**

Avoiding your task has the consequence that you become stressed and demotivated; being stressed is dangerous because you can feel tired and you will avoid your work in an endless vicious circle.

I wish to invite you to watch the hilarious and insightful video on YouTube about procrastination which the speaker Tim Urban has explained with a funny example: 'Inside the mind of a master procrastinator'.

## SOME HELP TO REDUCE THE FEAR OF SUCCESS.

The next workout can be used both by those who want to overcome the fear of failure and by those who want to reduce the fear of success.

- Check your motivation level with well-planned short-term goals.

- By achieving your short-term goals you will progress step by step along the road to success.

- Be aware of your words and thoughts. As you think you act.

**Workout 84**                                             **Date:**

Visualising your success, you can reduce your fears of achieving success with this exercise:

- Imagine you have achieved your goal.

- Imagine how you feel about it. Ask yourself what the positive and negative thoughts are. Write them down.

- Imagine how your goal could affect and impact on your life.

-   Think about the benefits of your goal.

- Talk to yourself and record your conversation, then use that record to be motivated and overcome your 'fear of success'.

*A short story about me that I want share with you.*

*In the last three years of my life many things have changed and many of these have left me incredulous. In fact, never in my life had I thought of writing a book, even less in English!*

*I wish to share with you, my dear reader, some events in my life which were initially sad and dramatic and then turned into opportunities for me.*

*It was in 2009 and I was working in a large supermarket in my beloved Alessandria, a quiet town in Piedmont in Italy when, as a result of the long hours worked and fatigue, I didn't have any spare time and I began to lose myself. I had given up many things, stupidly chasing purpose by working hard. As I was telling you, I lost contact with myself and started living without any sense of direction.*

*In the meantime I went to live alone. It was a need of the soul and I wanted to challenge myself in building a life by my own strength.*

*After a few months I met a girl and I do not hide the fact that I was very shy, but I made myself like a lion and stopped to talk to her. I was entranced by her beauty and blonde hair.*

*I lost track of time and spent three hours talking to her on a bench and I will never forget that magical time. After going out several times together our friendship became love, a love never felt in my life, a deep love, a love opposed by many people around us. Our life together was an alternation of moments of joy, tension and events that sabotaged our serenity.*

*One of these was my dismissal from the supermarket with one of the most cruel and inhumane actions. I had to sign a dismissal letter in my hand. I recognise that I made mistakes but I know that they were caused by my deep tiredness and the many years spent at work, sacrificing my life for nothing! My friend believes me I did not have the strength to react. I was too taken by personal problems and I wanted to be calm to continue to live my love story with my beloved.*

*Despite this sad moment I started looking inside myself. I had to face reality and understand what was important for me.*

*I succeeded thanks to the help of my parents, my sister and my beloved to overcome that painful time, and I found a new job as an agent in an estate agency. During that experience I learned from my esteemed boss Enzo a couple of sentences that helped me to improve myself, marking a turning point in my life. One of his favourite phrases was the following: 'Cristian, you have to work on the details! You have to break the hair in four!' And it was true. I applied myself better and found numerous apartments for sale in my area, coming to sell my first home after a few months. This event helped to give me strength and encouraged me to believe in myself. After all, I deserved it after all the suffering I had endured.*

*Although I loved my job I decided to leave it as the Italian economic crisis didn't allow me to earn enough. I found another temporary job, hoping to improve my budget a bit but this was my downfall, because it wasn't the job I really wanted. From this experience I learned a hard lesson of life: never force events or make your own moves without first having enough experience! I had not put into practice another precious teaching of my boss Enzo, a teaching that comes from Seneca: 'No wind is favourable for the sailor who does not know where to go.'*

*And it is true: if I had waited, to gain experience and resources, perhaps today I would be telling another story, but who can say?*

*Other troubles started, expenses increased, and I had to sell my new car and my off-road motorbike, a splendid Vertemati 500, to collect the money needed to pay my debts. I cleared all the debts and managed to pay the rent for the flat. Unfortunately, in the meantime my landlord decided to sell his entire property!*

*At that time I went to eat at the Caritas charity in my town. I did not want to weigh on my parents. And I must say that the food was not bad at all, indeed, it was very good, and I could even count on a dessert at the end of the meal. I will always remember with respect the people I met during those moments who, despite their problems, always gave me a smile... even if sometimes it was toothless!*

*That situation helped me to re-emerge from the mud and I began to read every book that was useful for my personal growth. I remember that moment, it was in the winter cold and in the cold of my room that, immersed in the darkness, I read thanks to a candle one of Napoleon Hill's masterpieces,* The Law of Success.

*I sold everything I could to buy food and with the money saved I bought two used English books by Martin Seligman and Dale Carnegie. I was entranced by those readings although I understood little, given my lack of knowledge of the English language. Those readings proved useful to me. Indeed, they helped me to overcome a sad moment in my life once more when my beloved decided to leave me for another man. I immediately reacted but after a few hours I returned to myself. I realised that she had made her own choice and even though I loved her I knew she was not mine, but she belonged to herself and as such she had to choose her own life.*

*That moment was terrible, after three years of pain, sacrifice and battles spent to find a new balance.*

*A lucky day can appear at any time of our life, and ever since I have been happy to have sipped a coffee at a bar. While I was drinking my coffee I read an interesting article on Life Coaching and how four women managed to change their lives and the lives of those close to them. That same evening I looked for information and phoned one of the women in the article. One of the Life Coaches at the Italian School of Life & Corporate Coaching replied to me with a kind voice. I asked anyone for useful information to feed my curiosity about Life Coaching.*

*Well, after that great moment, dear friend, I read eight books on the subject in just two months, amazing for a person like me who read very little and rarely.*

*The work I had found in the meantime did not guarantee me a living and so I decided to leave the job. This time it was my decision because I wanted to change my life!*

*With some money I had saved I attended a Life Coaching course with Dr. Luca Stanchieri in Milan in 2015. It was an important test for me. For years I had not read or studied anything seriously or with dedication. I also had to overcome my fear of not finishing the course. Well, I overcame all my fears thanks to my tenacity and to the support of all the wonderful people I met along the path we trod together during our training.*

*I had grown as a person and had even more confidence in myself, a determination which I had previously sidelined, but came out at the right time. I completed my course as a Life Coach and decided to challenge myself once again.*

*I was planning to also attend the Corporate Coaching course too and so I did. I spent hours and hours studying books on personal development and Life Coaching so as to organise my first public speech on coaching after just a month. Thanks to Laura and Giovanni of the Italian Labour Union in Alessandria, I had the opportunity to speak in front of an audience of fifty people for the first time in my life! I met Laura and Giovanni during my voluntary work as a driver for elderly people, the disabled and autistic boys, an experience that I will always carry with me in my heart, remembering all the volunteers who taught me the value of solidarity.*

*I also wanted to move to England and learn more English. Thanks to the patience and professionalism of Laura Ottone from Turin, Italy, I was able to realise my dream of starting my adventure in the UK as an au pair… at forty-three years of age!*

*Time passed quickly and soon it was time to pack up for England.*

*I was so happy and excited to meet my host family in Lillington, a nice village near Leamington Spa in Warwickshire. Once again life gave me the opportunity to learn something and I learned a lot from my little friend and his mother who brought up her honey angel with love and courage.*

*In Leamington Spa I found many new friends as I became a volunteer at Brunswick Community, the British Heart Foundation and Myton Hospice. During my residence in Warwickshire I started to walk every day; I had to save money and it was the only way to get around. After a few weeks I decided to do something crazy. I planned to walk from village to village and I visited the towns of Warwick, Coventry, Stoneleigh, Kenilworth and Stratford-upon-Avon... sometimes covering more than sixty kilometres in a day! It gave me another life lesson: I learned that it is possible to drive your mind and your body. Instead of allowing myself to catch a bus or train, I wanted to overcome my limits. I enjoyed being alone and I was delighted to see the lovely countryside, the sheep and the horses during my trips. I will be forever grateful to the farmer who accompanied me through the crop fields for a mile because I lost my way and I wasn't able to find the right route.*

*The months passed quickly but the memories will always remain clear in my mind and I will never forget my first swim in the icy waters when I had to swim with my young friend!*

*My vocation to become a Life Coach led me to leave Leamington Spa and my host family.*

*I had to get as close as possible to London where I would have many opportunities for study. For a few months I helped another family as an au pair and soon after I found work in one of the best schools in England, **Hinchley Wood Secondary School** in Surrey. I was immediately impressed by the welcome from everyone. I always felt encouraged to learn new tasks. The environment was friendly and there was a strong spirit of collaboration. I still work at this school as a caretaker, a job that I like even though it is hard;*

with it I can afford to live in dignity and pay for my studies.

I always thought of returning something to people for their help and support, so I decided to become a volunteer at Evolve Housing Plus, a charity that helps homeless people. For almost a year I travelled between Surbiton and Croydon and I cannot tell you how many times I used to take the train. I liked being with those people and sometimes I forgot that I had to go back to work!

After a while the distance began to be felt and I reluctantly had to leave my friends at Evolve, but my gratitude was still great and that was how I started a charity programme with GRIT, a charity that helps students achieve their goals at school and improve themselves as people. I was inspired by the energy of all the people involved in the Performance Coach project and seeing the students working for their goals was the most beautiful gift I could wish for.

*My desire to become a Life Coach became even greater as I met new people and reached new goals. It was Laura and her Orpington group who suggested that I find new goals and rediscover my talent, revitalise my empathy for people, and above all encouraged me to write my first public presentation on life coaching in English. I understood that I had to stay focused and work hard, choosing a strategy that was tailored to my expectations but achievable in a short time. I wondered what was necessary for my purpose and what the best way to start could be. Once again I found the answers I was looking for. I had to work in the area where I lived, making myself known both as a person and as a life coach. I used every opportunity to meet new people and I encouraged myself to get out of my comfort zone; it was a rewarding choice because I met Jose Ucar La Salvia, one of the most beautiful people I have ever met. He's not just a great business coach, but he's a friend with whom I share a lot of my future projects. Jose and Roy Keene supported me in writing the book that you are reading.*

*Dear friend, I hope this story of mine has not bored you but inspired you to look for your own path with conviction and tenacity, overcoming hard times and tempering the impatience to get everything done immediately. Remember: Success is what you expect it to be, and if you want it with a pure and childish spirit it will not scare you, it will guide you to meet yourself and meet new people who will support you and make your journey on the road to success unforgettable!*

*In conclusion, I wish to talk to you about my approach as Performance Personal Coach. I always believed that if I can help one person to improve his or her life this will have an enormous impact on other lives. I am following this principle every day giving my best to the people around me, both as a man and as a life coach. I like to imagine how our planet can become if all of us can live with this virtue. I prefer to see the good things that humanity has done instead of seeing the bad version of our history. This thought drives me when I must trust people especially when I have to decide to meet my clients or the people who need my support as volunteer for the first time. I prefer to be ready to be amazed by human inner resources rather than hide myself under false beliefs and judgements. I want to be genuine with the person in front of me, allowing myself to discover the others' personal story, future vision and their strengths.*

*Maybe my character and my coaching approach can be too much for a certain kind of people because I want to be clear, honest and direct. I am the coach who, if I see the possibility and the inner power in people, will want encourage them to achieve their goals, giving them the opportunity to change their lives. I can only work with people if there is the opportunity to create the space for a coaching relationship, where there is a performance that needs to be increased or improved following the same approach as in sport training but with a profound humanistic vision of the person, respecting his or her whole being as unique and unrepeatable. I invite you to start considering leaving your comfort zone to create a new incredible way of changing your life, discovering the best version of themselves that exists in this universe.*

# Resources.

www.scuoladicoaching.it

www.success.com

www.briantracy.com

www.the-coaching-academy.com

www.linehaninstitute.org

www.businessdictionary.com/definition/success.htm

https://publishnation.co.uk

If you wish to become a volunteer Performance Coach with the GRIT Charity in London: www.grit.org.uk

## Sources and Bibliography.

C. Peterson and M. Seligman: *Character Strengths and Virtues: A Handbook and Classification*, 2004. Published by American Psychological Association, Oxford University Press. - Laura Nash and Howard Stevenson: *Just Enough: Tools for Creating Success in Your Work and Life.* - Napoleon Hill: *The Law of Success.* - Dale Carnegie: *How to Win Friends and Influence People.* - Brian Tracy: *Eat the Frog! Get More of the Important Things Done -*

*Today!* Hodder Mobius, 2004 United Kingdom. - Stephen R. Covey: *The 7 Habits of Highly Effective People.* - Dr. Fuschia M. Sirois and Timothy A. Pychyl: *Procrastination, Health, and Well-Being,* 22/06/2016 Elsevier. - Marsha Linehan: *This One Moment: Skills for Everyday Mindfulness. - Opposite Action: Changing Emotions You Want to Change.*

Geoff Colvin: *Talent is Overrated. What Really Separates World-Class Performers from Everybody Else.* Nicholas Breakley Publishing, 2008 U.K. - Professor Greg Whyte OBE: *Achieve the Impossible. How to Overcome Challenges and Gain Success in Life, Work and Sport.* Bantam Press 2015. - Consultant Deborah A. Olson, PhD. Success: *The Psychology of Achievement. A Practical Guide to Unlocking Your Potential in Every Area of Life.* - Jeff Archer: *Coach Your Own Life. Break Down the Barriers to Success.* Hodder Education 2010. United Kingdom. - Linda Shrimpton: *Be Happy. A Spiritual Journey Including Insight About Ets and our Future!* Printed by Amazon, 2015

Luca Stanchieri: *Scopri le tue Potenzialità: Come Trasformare le tue Capacità Nascoste in Talenti con la Psicologia Positiva e il Coaching.* Editore Franco Angeli, 2008. - *Il Life Coaching. Una Nuova Tecnica al Servizio delle Potenzialità e della Creatività Individuale.* Editore Verdechiaro, 2014. - *Non c'è Problema! Come Sfruttare le Difficoltà per Esprimere il tuo Potenziale.* Edizioni BUR, Luglio 2016.

Dr. Roberto Cerè: *Business Intelligente* BUR Edizioni Maggio 2018 - Io ci sono, BUR Edizioni, Settembre 2016.- Storie Impossibili, Mind Edizioni, Aprile 2016.

Alberto Avetta: *Licenziato a 50 anni.* Settembre 2015, U. Soletti Editore.

### *Websites sources & quotes.*

www.lessonslearnedinlife.com

www.resources.scalingtheheights.com

www.mariecurie.org.uk

www.businessdictionary.com.

https://aninoogunjobi.com/2016/08/encouraging-quote-success-iceberg-joseph-valente-tweeted

Dear reader, would you like more information or leave feedback, suggestions or advice about my book?

Please, don't hesitate to contact me:

**www.cristiancairo.com**

I thank you in advance for your interest!

*Cristian Cairo*

I say thank you to my friend Stuart Scary who has taken a pic about me during a relaxing day on motorbike! (Back cover's picture).

L - #0120 - 020120 - C0 - 210/148/25 - PB - DID2729859